I0794363

A MEDITATIVE COMMENTARY ON THE NEW TESTAMENT

1 AND 2 CORINTHIANS: JESUS, CROSS, CHURCH

A MEDITATIVE COMMENTARY ON THE NEW TESTAMENT

1 AND 2 CORINTHIANS: JESUS, CROSS, CHURCH

By Earl Lavender

LEAFWOOD PUBLISHERS

1 AND 2 CORINTHIANS:
Jesus, Cross, Church

LEAFWOOD
PUBLISHERS

ISBN 978-0-89112-568-6

Printed in the United States of America

Cover design by Greg Jackson, Jackson Design Co., llc

For information contact:
Leafwood Publishers, Abilene, Texas
1-877-816-4455 toll free
www.leafwoodpublishers.com

08 09 10 11 12 13 / 7 6 5 4 3 2 1

To my brother Gary Holloway, a true scholar,
a wonderful co-worker in the kingdom, a faithful friend

ACKNOWLEDGEMENTS

I am deeply thankful to Gary Holloway for partnering with me in this effort. While this study in particular is dedicated to him, his help has been indispensable in every volume I've written in this series. I am also continually thankful to Leonard Allen and Leafwood Publishers. He is tireless in his work to expand the kingdom of God through the ministry of publishing and is a great encouragement and example to me.

I continue to be inspired by my brothers and sisters in the "early birds" Bible class. These precious saints have blessed and changed my life. I am also thankful to those who meet with Rebecca and me most Sunday evenings in our house church. Your faithfulness in the study of God's word is a constant encouragement.

As always, none of this work could be done without the wonderful and loving support of Rebecca. She has taught me more about the truth of Scripture than anyone else. Besides Jesus, she is my greatest blessing in this life. I will be forever in her debt for her actively living in God's love as my loving spouse. She is my constant inspiration.

CONTENTS

INTRODUCTION

1 CORINTHIANS

MEDITATIONS

2 CORINTHIANS

MEDITATIONS

INTRODUCTION:

HEARING GOD IN SCRIPTURE

There are many commentaries, guides, and workbooks on the various books of the Bible. How is this series different? It is not intended to answer all your scholarly questions about the Bible, or even make you an expert in the details of Scripture. Instead, this series is designed to help you hear the voice of God in your everyday life. It is a guide to meditation on the Bible, meditation that will allow the Bible to transform you.

We read in many ways. We might scan the newspaper for information, read a map for location, read a novel for pleasure, or read a textbook to pass a test. These are all good ways to read, depending on our circumstances.

A young soldier far away from home who receives a letter from his wife reads in yet another way. He might scan the letter quickly at first for news and information. But his longing for his beloved causes him to read the letter again and again, hearing her sweet voice in every line. He consciously treasures each word of this precious letter.

Bible Study

So also, there are many good ways to read the Bible, depending on our circumstances. Bible study is absolutely necessary for our life with God. We rightly study the Bible for information. We ask, "Who wrote this?" "When was it written?" "Who were the original readers?" "How do these words apply to me?" More importantly, we want information about God. Who is he? What does he think of me? What does he want from me?

There is no substitute for this kind of close, dedicated Bible study. We must know what the Bible says to know our standing with God. We therefore read the Bible to discover true doctrine or teaching. But some—in their emphasis on the authority and inspiration of the Bible—have forgotten that Bible study is not an end in itself. We want to know God through Scripture. We want to have a relationship with the Teacher, not just the teachings.

Jesus tells some of God's people in his day, "You diligently study the Scriptures because you think that by them you possess eternal life. These are the Scriptures that testify about me, yet you refuse to come to me to have life" (John 5:39-40). He's not telling them to study their Bibles less, but he is reminding them of the deeper purpose of Bible study—to draw us to God through Jesus. Bible study is a means, not an end.

Yet the way many of us have learned to study the Bible may actually get in the way of hearing God. "Bible study" may sound a lot like schoolwork, and many of us were happy to get out of school. "Bible study" may call to mind pictures of intellectuals surrounded by books in Greek and Hebrew, pondering meanings too deep for ordinary people. The method of Bible study that has been popular for some time focuses on the strangeness of the Bible. It was written long ago, far away, and in languages we cannot read. There is a huge gap between us and the original readers of the Bible, a gap that can only be bridged by scholars, not by average folk.

There is some truth and some value in that "scholarly" method. It is true that the Bible was not written originally to us. Knowing ancient languages and customs can at times help us understand the Bible better. However, one unintended result of this approach is to make the Bible distant from the people of God. We may come to think that we can only hear God indirectly through Scripture, that his word must be filtered through scholars. We may even think that deep Bible study is a matter of mastering obscure information about the Bible.

Meditation

But we read the Bible for more than information. By studying it, we experience transformation, the mysterious process of God at work in us. Through his loving words, God is calling us to life with him. He is forming us into the image of his Son.

Reading the Bible is not like reading other books. We are not simply trying to learn information or master material. Instead, we want to stand under the authority of Scripture and let God master us. While we read the Bible, it reads us, opening the depths of our being to the overpowering love of God. "For the word of God is living and active. Sharper than any doubleedged sword, it penetrates even to dividing soul and spirit, joints and marrow; it judges the thoughts and attitudes of the heart. Nothing in all creation is hidden from God's sight. Everything is uncovered and laid bare before the eyes of him to whom we must give account" (Hebrews 4:12-13).

Opening our hearts to the word of God is meditation. Although this way of reading the Bible may be new to some, it has a long heritage among God's people. The Psalmist joyously meditates on the words of God (Psalm 1:2; 39:3; 119:15, 23, 27, 48, 78, 97, 99, 148). Meditation is taking the words of Scripture to heart and letting them ask questions of us. It is slowly chewing over a text, listening closely, reading God's message of love to us over and over. This is not a simple, easy, or naïve reading of Scripture, but a process that takes time, dedication, and practice on our part.

There are many ways to meditate on the Bible. One is praying the Scriptures. Prayer and Bible study really cannot be separated. One way of praying the Bible is to make the words of a text your prayer. Obviously, the prayer texts of Scripture, especially the Psalms, lend themselves to this. "The Lord is my shepherd" has been the prayer of many hearts.

It is proper and helpful to turn the words of the Bible into prayers. Commands from God can become prayers. "You shall have no other gods before me" (Exodus 20:3) can be prayed, "Lord, keep me from anything that takes your place in my heart." Stories can be prayed. Jesus heals a man born blind (John 9), and so we pray, "Lord Jesus open my eyes to who you truly are." Even the promises of the Bible become prayers. "Never will I leave you; never will I forsake you" (Deuteronomy 31:6; Hebrews 13:5) becomes "God help me know that you promise that you are always with me and so live my life without fear."

Obviously, there are many helpful ways of hearing the voice of God in Scripture. Again, the purpose of Bible reading and study is not to know more about the Bible, much less to pride ourselves as experts on Scripture. Instead, we read to hear the voice of our Beloved. We listen for a word from God to us.

Holy Reading

This commentary reflects one ancient way of meditation and praying the Scriptures known as *lectio divina,* or holy reading. This method assumes that God wants to speak to us directly in the Bible, that the passage we are reading is God's word to us right now. The writers of the New Testament read the Old Testament with this same conviction. They saw the words of the Bible speaking directly to their own situation. They read with humility and with prayer.

The first step along this way of holy reading is listening to the Bible. Choose a biblical text that is not too long. This commentary breaks Paul's letters to the Corinthians into smaller sections. The purpose is to hear God's voice in your current situation, not to cover material or prepare lessons. Get into a comfortable position and maintain silence before God for several minutes. This prepares the heart to listen. Read slowly. Savor each word. Perhaps read aloud. Listen for a particular phrase that speaks to you. Ask God, "What are you trying to tell me today?"

The next step is to meditate on that particular phrase. That meditation may include slowly repeating the phrase that seems to be for you today. As you think deeply on it, you might even memorize it. Committing biblical passages to memory allows us to hold them in our hearts all day long. If you keep a journal, you might write the passage there. Let those words sink deeply into your heart.

Then pray those words back to God in your heart. Those words may call up visual images, smells, sounds, and feelings. Pay attention to what God is giving you in those words. Then respond in faith to what those words say to your heart. What do they call you to be and to do? Our humble response might take the form of praise, thanksgiving, joy, confession, or even cries of pain.

The final step in this "holy reading" is contemplation of God. The words from God that we receive deeply in our hearts lead us to him. Through these words, we experience union with the all-powerful God of love. And that encounter does not leave us unchanged. Contemplation leads us to kingdom action based on the reading. To what does this reading lead? What will I now do because of my deeper understanding of God's will for my life? Think of specific actions and make them a part of your daily walk.

What keeps reading the Bible this way from becoming merely our own desires read back into Scripture? How do we know it is God's voice we hear and not our own?

Consider two things. One is prayer. We are asking God to open our hearts, minds, and lives to him. We ask to hear his voice, not ours and not the voice of the world around us.

The second thing that keeps this from being an exercise in self-deception is to study the Bible in community. By praying over Scripture in a group, we hear God's word together. God speaks through the other members of our group. The wisdom he gives them keeps us from private, selfish, and unusual interpretations. They help us keep our own voices in check, as we desire to listen to God alone.

HOW TO USE THIS COMMENTARY

This commentary provides assistance in holy reading of the Bible. It gives structure to daily personal devotions, family meditation, small group Bible studies, and church classes.

Daily Devotional

Listening, meditation, prayer, contemplation—how does this commentary fit into this way of Bible study? Consider it as a conversation partner. We have taken a section of Scripture and then broken it down into four short daily readings. After listening, meditating, praying, and contemplating the passage for the day, use the questions suggested in the commentary to provoke deeper reflection. This provides a structure for a daily fifteen minute devotional four days a week. On the fifth day, read the entire passage, meditate, and then use the questions to reflect on the meaning of the whole. On day six, take our meditations on the passage as conversation with another who has prayed over the text.

If you want to begin daily Bible reading but need guidance, this provides a Monday-Saturday experience that prepares the heart for worship and praise on Sunday. This structure also results in a communal reading of Scripture, instead of a private reading. Even if you use this commentary alone, you are not reading privately. God is at work in you and in the conversation you have with another (the author of the commentary) who has sought to hear God through this particular passage of the Bible.

Family Bible Study

This commentary can also provide an arrangement for family Bible study. Many Christian parents want to lead their children in daily study but don't know where to begin or how to structure their time. Using the six-day plan outlined above means the entire family can read, meditate, pray, and reflect on the shorter passages, using the questions provided. On day five, they can review the entire passage, and then on day six, read the meditations in the commentary to prompt reflection and discussion. God will bless our families beyond our imaginations through the prayerful study of his word.

Weekly Group Study

This commentary can also structure small group Bible study. Each member of the group should have meditated over the daily readings and questions for the five days preceding the group meeting, using the method outlined above. The day before the group meeting, each member should read and reflect on the meditations in the commentary on that passage. You then can meet once a week to hear God's word together. In that group meeting, the method of holy reading would look something like this:

Listening

1. Five minutes of silence.
2. Slow reading of the biblical passage for that week.
3. A minute of silent meditation on the passage.
4. Briefly share with the group the word or phrase that struck you.

Personal Message

5. A second reading of the same passage.
6. A minute of silence.

7. Where does this touch your life today?
8. Responses: I hear, I see, etc.

Life Response

9. Brief silence.
10. What does God want you to do today in light of this text?

Group Prayer

11. Have each member of the group pray aloud for the person on his or her left, asking God to bless the word he has given them.

The procedure suggested here can be used in churches or in neighborhood Bible studies. Church members would use the daily readings Monday-Friday in their daily devotionals. This commentary intentionally provides no readings on the sixth day, so that we can spend Saturdays as a time of rest, not rest from Bible study, but a time to let God's word quietly work its way deep into our hearts. Sunday during Bible school or in home meetings, the group would meet to experience the weekly readings together, using the group method described above. It might be that the sermon for each Sunday could be on the passage for that week.

There are churches that have used this structure to great advantage. Members come to the worship assembly prepared to hear a word from God in that particular text. Much of the background information that is sometimes needed in a sermon has already been given. Preaching can be much more focused on a particular teaching. We strongly urge churches try this type of congregational approach to the study of God's word. In the hallways of those churches who have embraced this type of study, the talk is not of the local football team or the weather, but of the shared experience of the Word of God for that week.

And that is the purpose of our personal and communal study, to hear the voice of God, our loving Father who wants us to love him in return. He deeply desires a personal relationship with us. Father, Son, and Spirit make a home inside us (see John 14:16-17, 23). Our loving God speaks to his children! But we must listen for his voice. That listening is not a matter of gritting our teeth and trying harder to hear. Instead, it is part of our entire life with God. That is what Bible study is all about.

Through daily personal prayer and meditation on God's word, and through a communal reading of Scripture, our most important conversation partner—the Holy Spirit—will do his mysterious and marvelous work. Among other things, the Spirit pours God's love into our hearts (Romans 5:5), bears witness to our spirits that we are God's children (Romans 8:16), intercedes for us with God (Romans 8:26), and enlightens us as to God's will (Ephesians 1:17).

So this is an invitation to personal daily Bible study, to praying the Scriptures, to sharing with fellow believers, to hearing the voice of God. God will bless us, our families, our churches, and his world if we take the time to be still, listen, and be obedience to his word.

1 CORINTHIANS:

THE UNIFYING POWER OF JESUS CHRIST CRUCIFIED

THE SPIRITUALITY OF 1 CORINTHIANS

Surely the desire of every follower of Jesus is to glorify God in ever increasing ways. At times, this calls for a better understanding of God's will for us. At other times, it calls for repentance from things that do not belong in our lives or our churches. Paul's letters to the Corinthians demonstrate how these aspects of spiritual growth are interrelated. Simply exposing sin is important, but does not necessarily motivate one to repent. If, instead, a profound teaching is convincingly established which exposes sin as counter to God's purposes, then one has much motivation to change. And such repentance is not simply turning away from sin, but rather radically changing direction (repentance) in order to fully embrace the kingdom of God.

Thus the title of this commentary: "Jesus, Cross, Church." Paul's main objective in this letter was to establish the truth that Jesus Christ came to give the world *new life through his cross*, and that the church was the vehicle chosen to proclaim this life to the world. The church, by its very nature, was and is the proclamation and manifestation of God's living truth to a sinful world. Nothing must be allowed to distract the church from its central purpose.

UNITY THROUGH THE CROSS

One reading 1 Corinthians quickly encounters Paul's deepest concern. The church was struggling because of a lack of unity. Paul called them to embody the fundamental truth that in Christ Jesus they must be one. Jesus Christ came to demonstrate the power of God through full submission to his will leading to death on the cross. It was the power of this sacrifice which sanctified the believer and allowed for the indwelling of the Holy Spirit. These truths could only be proclaimed to the world through a *unified* church.

This unity could never be achieved through the use of worldly thinking. It could only be attained through the power of self-sacrificed, modeled in the cross of Christ. It was this model of power the Corinthians were to embrace, rather than the understandings of power prevalent in their contemporary culture—the power of the conquering armies of Rome or of each individual claiming worth and authority through earthly things. If each of the believers would follow Jesus Christ to the cross, unity would be restored and God would be glorified.

CONFRONTING SIN

Unity could not be enjoyed in the Corinthian church unless sins were confronted and repentance embraced. In this letter Paul dealt with sins having to do with human sexuality, divorce, disputes among believers, and appropriate behavior in assembly of the church. One of the great values of this text for us is to learn from Paul how to effectively confront sin and discord. For Paul, if a certain issue caused discord in the church, it was to be confronted. Even minor social questions were to be evaluated through that which would bring peace and unity—the cross of Jesus Christ.

LIVING OUT THE GOSPEL IN OUR CULTURE

Not only do we find valuable information on confronting sin, but Paul helps us consider a question of particular relevance. How do we faithfully live as disciples of Jesus Christ in *our* culture? This question will serve us well as we meditate on the content of this letter. Instead of seeking Paul's specific answers to particular cultural issues, let's seek to understand the theological roots and ethical implications of his responses. I doubt we will ever come to full agreement on how to appropriately respond to Paul's specific teachings concerning several of the issues he confronted in this letter (woman's role in the church, divorce, spiritual gifts, and others). The question for us, as we read and meditate on this letter, is "what would Paul identify as issues which need to be addressed in our lives and in our culture?" Is the power of Jesus Christ crucified seen in the way we confront sin and issues that divide us in the church?

MODELING THE GOSPEL

As we consider how this letter might impact our spiritual formation, one of the most compelling fundamentals of ministry exhibited is the power and necessity of example. Paul modeled what he called for in others, unafraid to identify his behavior with the Corinthians an example of "the power of the cross." Rather than appealing to his accomplishments (which he does in parody in 2 Corinthians), he modeled the power of "other-oriented" living. While his sarcasm and direct accusations may make us uncomfortable at times, the deep love he had for his "children in the faith" is beyond question. He desperately wanted them to live in a peaceful unity in the Holy Spirit, through the work of Jesus Christ, which would bring glory to God. All he had done while with them personally and through his writing modeled the truth to which he called them.

Paul opened this letter with a blessing of grace and peace, and closed it with a blessing of grace and love. In between, there are difficult issues to consider. May our study of this personal letter to a struggling church give us a deeper understanding of God's grace, peace, and love and help transform us into the image of Christ Jesus our Lord.

"Holy Father, we humbly pray that you lead us in this study to a deeper commitment to glorify you through embracing the power of a life fully submitted to you."

JESUS CHRIST AND THE CROSS

(1:1-2:5)

DAY ONE READING AND QUESTIONS

1 Paul, called to be an apostle of Christ Jesus by the will of God, and
our brother Sosthenes,

2 To the church of God in Corinth, to those sanctified in Christ Jesus
and called to be holy, together with all those everywhere who call on the
name of our Lord Jesus Christ—their Lord and ours:

3 Grace and peace to you from God our Father and the Lord Jesus
Christ.

4 I always thank God for you because of his grace given you in Christ
Jesus. 5 For in him you have been enriched in every way—in all your
speaking and in all your knowledge— 6 because our testimony about
Christ was confirmed in you. 7 Therefore you do not lack any spiritual gift
as you eagerly wait for our Lord Jesus Christ to be revealed. 8 He will keep
you strong to the end, so that you will be blameless on the day of our
Lord Jesus Christ. 9 God, who has called you into fellowship with his Son
Jesus Christ our Lord, is faithful.

1. *What did Paul identify as the purpose of the church of God in Corinth—who were they to be?*

2. *How had the Corinthians been enriched by God?*

3. *Whose faithfulness did Paul emphasize in his introduction? Why is that important to us?*

DAY TWO READING AND QUESTIONS

10 I appeal to you, brothers, in the name of our Lord Jesus Christ, that all of you agree with one another so that there may be no divisions among you and that you may be perfectly united in mind and thought. 11 My brothers, some from Chloe's household have informed me that there are quarrels among you. 12 What I mean is this: One of you says, "I follow Paul"; another, "I follow Apollos"; another, "I follow Cephas'"; still another, "I follow Christ."

13 Is Christ divided? Was Paul crucified for you? Were you baptized into the name of Paul? 14 I am thankful that I did not baptize any of you except Crispus and Gaius, 15 so no one can say that you were baptized into my name. 16 (Yes, I also baptized the household of Stephanas; beyond that, I don't remember if I baptized anyone else.) 17 For Christ did not send me to baptize, but to preach the gospel—not with words of human wisdom, lest the cross of Christ be emptied of its power.

1. *What was the problem Paul confronted in this letter?*

2. *Why do you think Paul asked if he (Paul) were crucified for them? What was his point?*

3. *What was Paul's primary obligation when among the Corinthians? Why do you think he pointed this out?*

DAY THREE READING AND QUESITONS

18 For the message of the cross is foolishness to those who are perishing, but to us who are being saved it is the power of God. 19 For it is written:

> "I will destroy the wisdom of the wise;
> the intelligence of the intelligent I will frustrate."

20 Where is the wise man? Where is the scholar? Where is the philosopher of this age? Has not God made foolish the wisdom of

the world? [21] For since in the wisdom of God the world through its
wisdom did not know him, God was pleased through the foolish-
ness of what was preached to save those who believe. [22] Jews demand
miraculous signs and Greeks look for wisdom, [23] but we preach Christ
crucified: a stumbling block to Jews and foolishness to Gentiles,
[24] but to those whom God has called, both Jews and Greeks, Christ the
power of God and the wisdom of God. [25] For the foolishness of God is
wiser than man's wisdom, and the weakness of God is stronger than
man's strength.

1. *How was the message of the cross foolishness to those who were perishing?*

2. *How has God made foolish the wisdom of the world?*

3. *In what sense was Christ the power and wisdom of God?*

DAY FOUR READING AND QUESTIONS

[26] Brothers, think of what you were when you were called. Not
many of you were wise by human standards; not many were influential;
not many were of noble birth. [27] But God chose the foolish things of
the world to shame the wise; God chose the weak things of the world
to shame the strong. [28] He chose the lowly things of this world and the
despised things—and the things that are not—to nullify the things that
are, [29] so that no one may boast before him. [30] It is because of him that
you are in Christ Jesus, who has become for us wisdom from God—that
is, our righteousness, holiness and redemption. [31] Therefore, as it is
written: "Let him who boasts boast in the Lord."

[2:1] When I came to you, brothers, I did not come with eloquence or
superior wisdom as I proclaimed to you the testimony about God. [2] For
I resolved to know nothing while I was with you except Jesus Christ
and him crucified. [3] I came to you in weakness and fear, and with much

trembling. [4] My message and my preaching were not with wise and persuasive words, but with a demonstration of the Spirit's power, [5] so that your faith might not rest on men's wisdom, but on God's power.

1. *Why did Paul remind the members of the church in Corinth that most of them lacked significance according to the standards of the world?*

2. *How are we to "boast in the Lord?"*

3. *Why did Paul resolve to know nothing except Jesus Christ and him crucified while among the Corinthians? Did he mean this literally? How did Paul manifest this?*

DAY FIVE READING AND QUESTIONS

Reread the entire text (1:1-20)

1. *In the context of our daily lives, how will those around us know that we are "sanctified in Christ" and "called to be holy?"*

2. *What does Paul see as the solution to divisions within the body? How might this approach to resolving divisions help today's church be unified?*

3. *How can we, with Paul, attempt to build faith not based on earthly wisdom but on God's power? How do we live in such a way that we manifest the power of the cross?*

MEDITATION

Do we know who we are in Christ? Paul considered this question central in addressing the lack of unity among the Corinthian believers. Paul's message is of great importance to us because we, too, have been sanctified and set apart for God's purposes. Are our lives reflections of our new identity in Christ Jesus? While we are not divided into camps identified with Paul, Cephas, and Apollos, we still fall into Satan's trap of identifying ourselves as sects of believers based on something or someone other than Jesus Christ. Paul saw no justification for sectarianism in the church of his day; would he see it any differently in ours?

The message of the cross continues to challenge each of us. How could it be that one executed as a criminal was demonstrating the true power of the omnipotent creator God? Paul went to great lengths to make sure this paradoxical message was not muted or lessened in any way. Manipulative language or impressive human reasoning would only get in the way of the message of the cross. It was not and is not subject to humankind's judgment. As hard as it is to accept, here is the truth: life cannot be authentically experienced without death. So Jesus died for us that we might find life. Our identities are totally dependent on his work. There is no room for boasting about anything but Jesus.

I wonder what others would see if they observed our lives over a period of time? Would they see a humble attitude, our weakness, fear and trembling, our complete dependence on the love and grace of God? Would they see the power of the cross of Christ through our lives? Or would our own pursuit of earthly power and wisdom mute the message? Paul clearly wanted his readers to remember the foundation of the teaching of Jesus: "If you want to follow me, deny yourself, pick up your cross, and follow me."

The power of God is only seen in the life of a self-denying cross carrier.

"Oh, Lord, please forgive us when we trust in worldly wisdom rather that in the power of the cross. May our lives be an active testimony to the power of Jesus Christ crucified."

GIFTS OF WISDOM: HUMAN DIVISIONS

(2:6-3:15)

DAY ONE READING AND QUESTIONS

[6] We do, however, speak a message of wisdom among the mature,
but not the wisdom of this age or of the rulers of this age, who are
coming to nothing. [7] No, we speak of God's secret wisdom, a wisdom
that has been hidden and that God destined for our glory before time
began. [8] None of the rulers of this age understood it, for if they had,
they would not have crucified the Lord of glory. [9] However, as it is
written:

"No eye has seen,
no ear has heard,
no mind has conceived
what God has prepared for those who love him"—
[10] but God has revealed it to us by his Spirit.

1. *Why did Paul want to make a distinction between worldly and godly wisdom?*

2. *What kind of wisdom do you trust most—that of the world or that from God?*

3. *How is God's wisdom destined for our glory?*

DAY TWO READING AND QUESTIONS

The Spirit searches all things, even the deep things of God. 11 For
who among men knows the thoughts of a man except the man's spirit
within him? In the same way no one knows the thoughts of God except
the Spirit of God. 12 We have not received the spirit of the world but the
Spirit who is from God, that we may understand what God has freely
given us. 13 This is what we speak, not in words taught us by human
wisdom but in words taught by the Spirit, expressing spiritual truths in
spiritual words. 14 The man without the Spirit does not accept the things
that come from the Spirit of God, for they are foolishness to him, and he
cannot understand them, because they are spiritually discerned. 15 The
spiritual man makes judgments about all things, but he himself is not
subject to any man's judgment:

> 16 "For who has known the mind of the Lord
> that he may instruct him?"
> But we have the mind of Christ.

1. *What is the "spirit of man" of which Paul speaks?*

2. *What role does the Holy Spirit play in our understanding the true wisdom of God?*

3. *According to Paul, what can an individual understand about God if not assisted by the Holy Spirit?*

DAY THREE READING AND QUESTIONS

1 Brothers, I could not address you as spiritual but as worldly—mere
infants in Christ. 2 I gave you milk, not solid food, for you were not yet
ready for it. Indeed, you are still not ready. 3 You are still worldly. For since
there is jealousy and quarreling among you, are you not worldly? Are
you not acting like mere men? 4 For when one says, "I follow Paul," and
another, "I follow Apollos," are you not mere men?

[5] What, after all, is Apollos? And what is Paul? Only servants,
through whom you came to believe—as the Lord has assigned to each his
task. [6] I planted the seed, Apollos watered it, but God made it grow. [7] So
neither he who plants nor he who waters is anything, but only God, who
makes things grow. [8] The man who plants and the man who waters have
one purpose, and each will be rewarded according to his own labor. [9] For
we are God's fellow workers; you are God's field, God's building.

1. *Why do you think Paul scolded the Corinthian believers for being "still worldly?" Are we guilty of this? If so, in what ways?*

2. *What behaviors of the Corinthians convinced Paul that they were still worldly?*

3. *What did Paul see as his role in advancing God's kingdom? What does this tell us about Paul?*

DAY FOUR READING AND QUESTIONS

[10] By the grace God has given me, I laid a foundation as an expert
builder, and someone else is building on it. But each one should be
careful how he builds. [11] For no one can lay any foundation other than
the one already laid, which is Jesus Christ. [12] If any man builds on this
foundation using gold, silver, costly stones, wood, hay or straw, [13] his
work will be shown for what it is, because the Day will bring it to light. It
will be revealed with fire, and the fire will test the quality of each man's
work. [14] If what he has built survives, he will receive his reward. [15] If it is
burned up, he will suffer loss; he himself will be saved, but only as one
escaping through the flames.

1. *What was the only foundation possible, according to Paul?*

2. *What do you think Paul meant by building on the foundation of Jesus with "gold, silver, costly stones"? Identify specific examples of such materials in one's life.*

3. *How can the unwise builder survive, yet suffer great loss?*

DAY FIVE READING AND QUESTIONS

Reread the entire text (2:6-3:15)

1. *How can we better tune our hearts to hear the Spirit of God rather than being influenced by the wisdom of the world?*

2. *What materials are you using in your life to build on the foundation of Jesus Christ?*

3. *What is our role in our time and place in God's continuing work?*

MEDITATION

How can we, with our limited, finite minds, understand the infinite wisdom of God? We simply cannot. But God has taken care of our severe limitations by granting us the amazing gift of his Spirit who dwells in us. This is God's Spirit, who knows God intimately. The Spirit knows the deepest thoughts of God—and is given freely to us! The result is that we speak not with human wisdom, but with wisdom from the heart of God. Otherwise, how could we understand the meaning and power of the cross? We have been given the mind of Christ, an amazing gift, so that we might understand and do the will of God.

Paul lamented that he could not engage the Corinthian Christians in the deeper truths of God because they were still immersed in the world's philosophy of life. How could Paul say such a thing? They were fighting with each other. They were jealous of one another. If the Spirit were guiding them, they would be enjoying love and peace, forgiveness and true unity.

Dare we consider how Paul would see us? Are we showing the power of the Spirit of God through our communities of faith? Do our interactions with each other bear witness to the love of Christ Jesus and the peace of God's Spirit? When we understand how important our calling as the church truly is, we cannot tolerate worldly behaviors. We are the temple of God, and the world will never know him if we do not live by the guidance of his Spirit.

Is there a more basic question to consider than Paul's concerning the construction materials of our lives? There is no foundation for life other than Christ Jesus himself. God has given each of us this unmovable and perfect platform upon which to build our lives. What are we using with which to build our lives? Are we wasting our time constructing things that will not survive the fires of judgment? Wouldn't it be crushing to realize we spent our precious gift of a life purchased by the blood of Jesus building worthless things?

We boast in the cross of Christ by accepting the challenge to build on his foundation with eternal materials—a life of giving ourselves for the good of others. A life of imitating Jesus Christ crucified.

"Our Father, thank you for the indescribable gift of your Holy Spirit. May we learn to quiet our minds and rid them of the vain philosophies of our world so that we might hear the voice of your Spirit. May we discern what is of true value so that our lives are spent building with materials which bring glory to you."

SERVANT APOSTLES

(3:16-4:21)

DAY ONE READING AND QUESTION

16 Don't you know that you yourselves are God's temple and that God's Spirit lives in you? 17 If anyone destroys God's temple, God will destroy him; for God's temple is sacred, and you are that temple.

18 Do not deceive yourselves. If any one of you thinks he is wise by the standards of this age, he should become a "fool" so that he may become wise. 19 For the wisdom of this world is foolishness in God's sight. As it is written: "He catches the wise in their craftiness"; 20 and again, "The Lord knows that the thoughts of the wise are futile." 21 So then, no more boasting about men! All things are yours, 22 whether Paul or Apollos or Cephas or the world or life or death or the present or the future—all are yours, 23 and you are of Christ, and Christ is of God.

1. What or who did Paul identify as "God's temple?"

2. How does one "become a fool" that "he may be wise"?

3. Why is boasting about human accomplishments so inappropriate?

DAY TWO READING AND QUESTIONS

1 So then, men ought to regard us as servants of Christ and as those entrusted with the secret things of God. 2 Now it is required that those who have been given a trust must prove faithful. 3 I care very little if I

am judged by you or by any human court; indeed, I do not even judge myself. 4 My conscience is clear, but that does not make me innocent. It is the Lord who judges me. 5 Therefore judge nothing before the appointed time; wait till the Lord comes. He will bring to light what is hidden in darkness and will expose the motives of men's hearts. At that time each will receive his praise from God.

6 Now, brothers, I have applied these things to myself and Apollos for your benefit, so that you may learn from us the meaning of the saying, "Do not go beyond what is written." Then you will not take pride in one man over against another. 7 For who makes you different from anyone else? What do you have that you did not receive? And if you did receive it, why do you boast as though you did not?

1. *How did Paul want the church to regard him, Apollos, and others?*

2. *Why did Paul refuse the judgment of "human courts"?*

3. *What was Paul calling for in this context when he instructed his readers, "Do not go beyond what is written?"*

DAY THREE READING AND QUESTIONS

8 Already you have all you want! Already you have become rich! You have become kings—and that without us! How I wish that you really had become kings so that we might be kings with you! 9 For it seems to me that God has put us apostles on display at the end of the procession, like men condemned to die in the arena. We have been made a spectacle to the whole universe, to angels as well as to men. 10 We are fools for Christ, but you are so wise in Christ! We are weak, but you are strong! You are honored, we are dishonored! 11 To this very hour we go hungry and thirsty, we are in rags, we are brutally treated, we are homeless. 12 We work hard with our own hands. When we are cursed, we bless; when we are persecuted, we endure it; 13 when we are slandered, we answer kindly.

Up to this moment we have become the scum of the earth, the refuse of the world.

1. *Why did Paul use sarcasm in his dealings with the Corinthian believers?*

2. *When is it appropriate to use sarcasm—or it is appropriate?*

3. *What was the point of Paul's comparison of how some Christians saw him versus how they saw themselves?*

DAY FOUR READING AND QUESTIONS

[14] I am not writing this to shame you, but to warn you, as my dear
children. [15] Even though you have ten thousand guardians in Christ,
you do not have many fathers, for in Christ Jesus I became your father
through the gospel. [16] Therefore I urge you to imitate me. [17] For this
reason I am sending to you Timothy, my son whom I love, who is faithful
in the Lord. He will remind you of my way of life in Christ Jesus, which
agrees with what I teach everywhere in every church.

[18] Some of you have become arrogant, as if I were not coming to
you. [19] But I will come to you very soon, if the Lord is willing, and then
I will find out not only how these arrogant people are talking, but what
power they have. [20] For the kingdom of God is not a matter of talk but of
power. [21] What do you prefer? Shall I come to you with a whip, or in love
and with a gentle spirit?

1. *How could Paul appeal to his readers as their "father through the gospel?"*

2. *How was it that the Corinthian Christians were to imitate Paul? How are we to imitate Paul?*

3. *What would determine whether Paul's opponents had true power?*

DAY FIVE READING AND QUESTIONS

Reread the entire text (3:16- 4:21)

1. *Do you think people in churches today see themselves as God's temple—the place where his Spirit dwells? Why or why not?*

2. *How can we learn to see people as God sees them rather than subjecting them to our judgment?*

3. *How can we avoid the trap of attempting to improve our image (according to worldly values) rather than deepening our dependency on God?*

MEDITATION

Paul wanted his readers to see the importance of their lives in the context of God's purposes. The church was and continues to be the temple of God. The problem for some to whom Paul wrote was that they continued to be satisfied with worldly callings rather than pursuing the incomparably higher calling of God. Might this continue to be a problem for us? He has chosen us to be the place of his earthly dwelling! There can be no greater calling than this. We need to remind ourselves of this high calling on a daily basis. Otherwise, we will follow the meaningless path set by our world.

As the active temple of God in this world, our core understanding of life is dramatically changed. We no longer see things and people as the world does. We see worldly wisdom for the foolishness it truly is. How ridiculous would it be to embrace foolishness when the wisdom of God had been made available to us? It was this that had so upset Paul. His biting sarcasm shows us how deeply wounded he was by the stubbornness of the Corinthian believers to hold on to worldly thinking. Rather than representing the power of the cross, they were demonstrating their participation in the fallen power game of imperial Rome.

Before we are too hard on the Corinthians, we need to ask ourselves where we stand on this core issue. To whom do we entrust our lives? What are we pursuing in our lives? Do we seek power over others or do we look for opportunities to serve those who have nothing to give in return? Would Paul accuse us of trusting in the world instead of trusting God? If Paul were to come to us, would he come thankful for our faithful service witnessing to the power of the cross, or chide us over our worldliness? Would he come with a rod of discipline or in love and with a gentle spirit?

"Loving God, forgive us of our worldly arrogance and pride. Break our hearts so that we might humble ourselves before you and find the meaningful life you desire for us."

IMMORALITY? LAWSUITS?

(5:1- 6:20)

DAY ONE READING AND QUESTIONS

1 It is actually reported that there is sexual immorality among you,
and of a kind that does not occur even among pagans: A man has his
father's wife. 2 And you are proud! Shouldn't you rather have been filled
with grief and have put out of your fellowship the man who did this?
3 Even though I am not physically present, I am with you in spirit. And I
have already passed judgment on the one who did this, just as if I were
present. 4 When you are assembled in the name of our Lord Jesus and I
am with you in spirit, and the power of our Lord Jesus is present, 5 hand
this man over to Satan, so that the sinful nature may be destroyed and
his spirit saved on the day of the Lord.

6 Your boasting is not good. Don't you know that a little yeast works
through the whole batch of dough? 7 Get rid of the old yeast that you
may be a new batch without yeast—as you really are. For Christ, our
Passover lamb, has been sacrificed. 8 Therefore let us keep the Festival,
not with the old yeast, the yeast of malice and wickedness, but with
bread without yeast, the bread of sincerity and truth.

9 I have written you in my letter not to associate with sexually
immoral people— 10 not at all meaning the people of this world who
are immoral, or the greedy and swindlers, or idolaters. In that case you
would have to leave this world. 11 But now I am writing you that you must
not associate with anyone who calls himself a brother but is sexually
immoral or greedy, an idolater or a slanderer, a drunkard or a swindler.
With such a man do not even eat.

[12] What business is it of mine to judge those outside the church? Are you not to judge those inside? [13] God will judge those outside. "Expel the wicked man from among you."

1. *What kind of human reasoning would allow the Corinthian believers to be proud about sin in their church?*

2. *How was it that Paul was clearly judging this situation in Corinth? Didn't Jesus say to "judge not?"*

3. *What was the festival Paul called his readers to keep with the bread of sincerity and truth? What does this mean to us?*

DAY TWO READING AND QUESTIONS

[1] If any of you has a dispute with another, dare he take it before the
ungodly for judgment instead of before the saints? [2] Do you not know
that the saints will judge the world? And if you are to judge the world,
are you not competent to judge trivial cases? [3] Do you not know that we
will judge angels? How much more the things of this life! [4] Therefore, if
you have disputes about such matters, appoint as judges even men of
little account in the church! [5] I say this to shame you. Is it possible that
there is nobody among you wise enough to judge a dispute between
believers? [6] But instead, one brother goes to law against another—and
this in front of unbelievers!

[7] The very fact that you have lawsuits among you means you have
been completely defeated already. Why not rather be wronged? Why not
rather be cheated? [8] Instead, you yourselves cheat and do wrong, and you
do this to your brothers.

1. *How did Paul think disputes within the church should be resolved?*

2. *Why was it inappropriate for disputes among Christians to be settled "in front of unbelievers?"*

3. *Ultimately, what did Paul suggest one do if wrongs involving brothers and sisters in the Lord cannot be resolved? Are you willing to do this? Why or why not?*

DAY THREE READING AND QUESTIONS

[9] Do you not know that the wicked will not inherit the kingdom of
God? Do not be deceived: Neither the sexually immoral nor idolaters nor
adulterers nor male prostitutes nor homosexual offenders [10] nor thieves
nor the greedy nor drunkards nor slanderers nor swindlers will inherit
the kingdom of God. [11] And that is what some of you were. But you were
washed, you were sanctified, you were justified in the name of the Lord
Jesus Christ and by the Spirit of our God.

1. *Who will not inherit the kingdom of God? Why?*

2. *What does this passage tell us about the background of some of the Corinthian Christians?*

3. *How were they freed from their past? Are you freed from you past?*

DAY FOUR READING AND QUESTIONS

[12] "Everything is permissible for me"—but not everything is benefi-
cial. "Everything is permissible for me"—but I will not be mastered by
anything. [13] "Food for the stomach and the stomach for food"—but God
will destroy them both. The body is not meant for sexual immorality,
but for the Lord, and the Lord for the body. [14] By his power God raised
the Lord from the dead, and he will raise us also. [15] Do you not know
that your bodies are members of Christ himself? Shall I then take the
members of Christ and unite them with a prostitute? Never! [16] Do you
not know that he who unites himself with a prostitute is one with her in

body? For it is said, "The two will become one flesh." [17] But he who unites
himself with the Lord is one with him in spirit.

[18] Flee from sexual immorality. All other sins a man commits are
outside his body, but he who sins sexually sins against his own body.
[19] Do you not know that your body is a temple of the Holy Spirit, who is
in you, whom you have received from God? You are not your own; [20] you
were bought at a price. Therefore honor God with your body.

1. *What is the difference between something that is permissible and something that is beneficial?*

2. *How is it that the body is for the Lord and the Lord for the body?*

3. *How are we to honor God with our bodies?*

DAY FIVE READING AND QUESTIONS

Reread the entire text (5:1- 6:20)

1. *Do you know of anyone who actually boasted in a particular sin? Have you ever done this? How do we avoid such behavior?*

2. *How are we to identify and deal with sinful living within our communities of faith?*

3. *How should understanding our bodies as the temple of God's Holy Spirit influence our behavior?*

MEDITATION

One of the great dilemmas in the biblical story is how a sinless, perfect, holy God can dwell among a sinful, flawed, and unholy people. As believers, we understand that this is the reason Jesus Christ came to this world. He is God's ultimate gift to humankind. Through his blood we are cleansed of our sins, forgiven, and God's Holy Spirit can take up residence in us. We are the temple of God. It is not enough just to believe the story; we must live in its truth.

What, then, do we do with a believer living in sin? Surely we would not boast of it. But would we confront it in a way that would ultimately proclaim the message of the cross? This is not so much about punishing the sinner as making the church the dwelling of God it is intended to be. Those living in rebellion to God have no place as a part of his temple.

While we may not be involved in sin quite as scandalous as the one in Corinth, I wonder what Paul would tell us if he were to observe our lives. Do we understand the importance of our own decisions concerning behavior? Does our understanding of being God's temple direct our actions? Do we take seriously the ethical implications of what we choose to do with our bodies? We surely know of the dangers of sexual immorality and drunkenness—but what of greed (always wanting more), idolatry (desiring any person or thing more than God), slander (harming others with our words), swindling (taking advantage of others, misrepresenting the truth in dealing with others), or suing in order to get our way? In Paul's understanding, there were no minor sins. Sin, in any form, demonstrates a turning away from the message of the cross. If we are unwilling to confront those sins among us that raise ridicule even among nonbelievers, we have no understanding of the high calling of God's church.

"God of grace, may we see our bodies as vessels to be used to bring glory to you. Give us the strength to flee from any behavior that dishonors you and the wisdom to confront sinful behavior in your church."

MARRIAGE

(7:1-40)

DAY ONE READING AND QUESTIONS

[1] Now for the matters you wrote about: It is good for a man not to marry. [2] But since there is so much immorality, each man should have his own wife, and each woman her own husband. [3] The husband should fulfill his marital duty to his wife, and likewise the wife to her husband. [4] The wife's body does not belong to her alone but also to her husband. In the same way, the husband's body does not belong to him alone but also to his wife. [5] Do not deprive each other except by mutual consent and for a time, so that you may devote yourselves to prayer. Then come together again so that Satan will not tempt you because of your lack of self-control. [6] I say this as a concession, not as a command. [7] I wish that all men were as I am. But each man has his own gift from God; one has this gift, another has that.

[8] Now to the unmarried and the widows I say: It is good for them to stay unmarried, as I am. [9] But if they cannot control themselves, they should marry, for it is better to marry than to burn with passion.

1. *Why did Paul suggest it was good for a person not to marry?*

2. *Paul had already written that one's body belonged to God. At this point in the letter, he taught that one's body belonged to one's spouse. How do you reconcile these teachings?*

3. *What advice did Paul give to the unmarried and the widows? Why?*

DAY TWO READING AND QUESTIONS

10 To the married I give this command (not I, but the Lord): A wife
must not separate from her husband. 11 But if she does, she must remain
unmarried or else be reconciled to her husband. And a husband must
not divorce his wife.

12 To the rest I say this (I, not the Lord): If any brother has a wife
who is not a believer and she is willing to live with him, he must not
divorce her. 13 And if a woman has a husband who is not a believer and
he is willing to live with her, she must not divorce him. 14 For the unbe-
lieving husband has been sanctified through his wife, and the unbelieving
wife has been sanctified through her believing husband. Otherwise your
children would be unclean, but as it is, they are holy.

15 But if the unbeliever leaves, let him do so. A believing man or
woman is not bound in such circumstances; God has called us to live in
peace. 16 How do you know, wife, whether you will save your husband? Or,
how do you know, husband, whether you will save your wife?

1. *What was Paul's command to the married?*

2. *What was Paul's teaching for those married to unbelievers?*

3. *What did Paul hope would happen in marriages of believers with unbelievers?*

DAY THREE READING AND QUESTIONS

17 Nevertheless, each one should retain the place in life that the Lord
assigned to him and to which God has called him. This is the rule I lay
down in all the churches. 18 Was a man already circumcised when he was
called? He should not become uncircumcised. Was a man uncircumcised
when he was called? He should not be circumcised. 19 Circumcision is
nothing and uncircumcision is nothing. Keeping God's commands is
what counts. 20 Each one should remain in the situation which he was

in when God called him. 21 Were you a slave when you were called?
Don't let it trouble you—although if you can gain your freedom, do so.
22 For he who was a slave when he was called by the Lord is the Lord's
freedman; similarly, he who was a free man when he was called is Christ's
slave. 23 You were bought at a price; do not become slaves of men.
24 Brothers, each man, as responsible to God, should remain in the situa-
tion God called him to.

25 Now about virgins: I have no command from the Lord, but I give
a judgment as one who by the Lord's mercy is trustworthy. 26 Because
of the present crisis, I think that it is good for you to remain as you are.
27 Are you married? Do not seek a divorce. Are you unmarried? Do not
look for a wife. 28 But if you do marry, you have not sinned; and if a
virgin marries, she has not sinned. But those who marry will face many
troubles in this life, and I want to spare you this.

29 What I mean, brothers, is that the time is short. From now on
those who have wives should live as if they had none; 30 those who
mourn, as if they did not; those who are happy, as if they were not; those
who buy something, as if it were not theirs to keep; 31 those who use the
things of the world, as if not engrossed in them. For this world in its
present form is passing away.

1. *What did Paul mean by retaining the place in life that the Lord has assigned?*

2. *What really matters in one's life?*

3. *What troubles do you think Paul anticipated for those entering married life?*

DAY FOUR READING AND QUESTIONS

32 I would like you to be free from concern. An unmarried man is
concerned about the Lord's affairs—how he can please the Lord. 33 But a

married man is concerned about the affairs of this world—how he can
please his wife— 34 and his interests are divided. An unmarried woman
or virgin is concerned about the Lord's affairs: Her aim is to be devoted
to the Lord in both body and spirit. But a married woman is concerned
about the affairs of this world—how she can please her husband. 35 I am
saying this for your own good, not to restrict you, but that you may live
in a right way in undivided devotion to the Lord.

36 If anyone thinks he is acting improperly toward the virgin he is
engaged to, and if she is getting along in years and he feels he ought
to marry, he should do as he wants. He is not sinning. They should get
married. 37 But the man who has settled the matter in his own mind, who
is under no compulsion but has control over his own will, and who has
made up his mind not to marry the virgin—this man also does the right
thing. 38 So then, he who marries the virgin does right, but he who does
not marry her does even better.

39 A woman is bound to her husband as long as he lives. But if her
husband dies, she is free to marry anyone she wishes, but he must belong
to the Lord. 40 In my judgment, she is happier if she stays as she is—and
I think that I too have the Spirit of God.

1. *What did Paul see as the advantage for the unmarried?*

2. *What was Paul asking those considering marriage to use as the basis for their decision?*

3. *If one's spouse died, what was Paul's advice? Why?*

DAY FIVE READING AND QUESTIONS

Reread the entire text (7:1-40)

1. *How should we view Paul's teaching concerning marriage? Does it apply directly to our situation?*

2. *If married to an unbeliever, what are ways the believing spouse can positively influence the other to God's glory?*

3. *What do you think of Paul's advice to "retain the place in life that the Lord assigned"? How does this apply to us?*

MEDITATION

How do we live out the cross of Christ in our culture and in our relationships? What does it mean to proclaim "Jesus Christ crucified" as we confront the contemporary issues challenging our faith? In chapters 7-14, Paul answered specific questions dealing with the cultural circumstances of the Corinthian believers. Some of these questions are relevant for us, others involve issues particular to first-century Corinth.

Paul's teaching in this week's reading was significantly affected by a particular crisis. Whatever the crisis, it presented particular challenges to marriage and relationships. Paul was not opposed to marriage. However, under the circumstances he felt it was better not to marry. If Paul's counsel addressed a situation long past, how can his teachings be helpful to us today?

Perhaps it is best to return to the central question of the letter. How does one faithfully live out Christ crucified in the particular circumstances of one's life? Cultural situations change, basic principles of truth do not. Are you single? Do you wish to remain that way? Is that the best way to live out "Christ crucified" in your life? Paul's advice to you would be to remain single. Have you found someone you love deeply and to whom you are willing to join your life until death? Does marriage present to you the best opportunity to live "Christ crucified?" Then Paul would encourage you to marry.

Paul's teaching and personal advice to the Corinthians was not complex. They were to learn to live with undivided loyalty and devotion to God in the situation in which they found themselves. That is wonderful counsel. Living Christ crucified means we live for God's glory, not for what we want or for that which makes us happy. One does not necessarily exclude the other, but one will be valued over the other. What is our primary concern—God's will or our happiness?

Are you fully faithful to God in the present situation of your life? This is a choice; it is a spiritual discipline to make the decision to see your present circumstances as God's calling. If other opportunities present themselves, make the decision based on God's purposes for life. Paul reminded the Corinthians of something we seldom consider: "this world in its present form is passing away." Live for what will last.

"Sovereign God, give us the wisdom to make decisions that honor you. May we accept with grace the situation in which we live, giving you our undivided loyalty."

PREACH THE GOSPEL IN ALL THAT YOU DO

(8:1-9:27)

DAY ONE READING AND QUESTIONS

1 Now about food sacrificed to idols: We know that we all possess
knowledge. Knowledge puffs up, but love builds up. 2 The man who
thinks he knows something does not yet know as he ought to know. 3 But
the man who loves God is known by God.

4 So then, about eating food sacrificed to idols: We know that an
idol is nothing at all in the world and that there is no God but one. 5 For
even if there are so-called gods, whether in heaven or on earth (as indeed
there are many "gods" and many "lords"), 6 yet for us there is but one
God, the Father, from whom all things came and for whom we live; and
there is but one Lord, Jesus Christ, through whom all things came and
through whom we live.

7 But not everyone knows this. Some people are still so accustomed
to idols that when they eat such food they think of it as having been
sacrificed to an idol, and since their conscience is weak, it is defiled. 8 But
food does not bring us near to God; we are no worse if we do not eat,
and no better if we do.

1. What is the difference between knowledge and love?

2. What did idols mean to Paul?

3. What did Paul point out that believers know about God and Jesus Christ that others do not know? Why is this important?

DAY TWO READING AND QUESTIONS

9 Be careful, however, that the exercise of your freedom does not
become a stumbling block to the weak. 10 For if anyone with a weak
conscience sees you who have this knowledge eating in an idol's temple,
won't he be emboldened to eat what has been sacrificed to idols? 11 So
this weak brother, for whom Christ died, is destroyed by your knowledge.
12 When you sin against your brothers in this way and wound their weak
conscience, you sin against Christ. 13 Therefore, if what I eat causes my
brother to fall into sin, I will never eat meat again, so that I will not cause
him to fall.

1. How might our exercise of freedom cause others to stumble?

2. How can we destroy a weak brother or sister with our knowledge?

3. What was Paul's concern for brothers and sisters who are weak? How should this affect our thinking about young or weak Christians?

DAY THREE READING AND QUESTIONS

9:1 Am I not free? Am I not an apostle? Have I not seen Jesus our
Lord? Are you not the result of my work in the Lord? 2 Even though I
may not be an apostle to others, surely I am to you! For you are the seal
of my apostleship in the Lord.

3 This is my defense to those who sit in judgment on me. 4 Don't
we have the right to food and drink? 5 Don't we have the right to take
a believing wife along with us, as do the other apostles and the Lord's

brothers and Cephas? 6 Or is it only I and Barnabas who must work
for a living?

7 Who serves as a soldier at his own expense? Who plants a vineyard
and does not eat of its grapes? Who tends a flock and does not drink of
the milk? 8 Do I say this merely from a human point of view? Doesn't
the Law say the same thing? 9 For it is written in the Law of Moses: "Do
not muzzle an ox while it is treading out the grain." Is it about oxen
that God is concerned? 10 Surely he says this for us, doesn't he? Yes, this
was written for us, because when the plowman plows and the thresher
threshes, they ought to do so in the hope of sharing in the harvest. 11 If
we have sown spiritual seed among you, is it too much if we reap a mate-
rial harvest from you? 12 If others have this right of support from you,
shouldn't we have it all the more?

But we did not use this right. On the contrary, we put up with
anything rather than hinder the gospel of Christ. 13 Don't you know that
those who work in the temple get their food from the temple, and those
who serve at the altar share in what is offered on the altar? 14 In the same
way, the Lord has commanded that those who preach the gospel should
receive their living from the gospel.

1. *What right was Paul justifying with his metaphor of sharing the harvest?*

2. *Why didn't Paul use the right for which he argued here?*

3. *In what way should those preaching the gospel receive their living from the gospel?*

DAY FOUR READING AND QUESTIONS

15 But I have not used any of these rights. And I am not writing this
in the hope that you will do such things for me. I would rather die than
have anyone deprive me of this boast. 16 Yet when I preach the gospel, I

cannot boast, for I am compelled to preach. Woe to me if I do not preach
the gospel! 17 If I preach voluntarily, I have a reward; if not voluntarily,
I am simply discharging the trust committed to me. 18 What then is my
reward? Just this: that in preaching the gospel I may offer it free of charge,
and so not make use of my rights in preaching it.

19 Though I am free and belong to no man, I make myself a slave to
everyone, to win as many as possible. 20 To the Jews I became like a Jew,
to win the Jews. To those under the law I became like one under the law
(though I myself am not under the law), so as to win those under the
law. 21 To those not having the law I became like one not having the law
(though I am not free from God's law but am under Christ's law), so as to
win those not having the law. 22 To the weak I became weak, to win the
weak. I have become all things to all men so that by all possible means
I might save some. 23 I do all this for the sake of the gospel, that I may
share in its blessings.

24 Do you not know that in a race all the runners run, but only
one gets the prize? Run in such a way as to get the prize. 25 Everyone
who competes in the games goes into strict training. They do it to get a
crown that will not last; but we do it to get a crown that will last forever.
26 Therefore I do not run like a man running aimlessly; I do not fight
like a man beating the air. 27 No, I beat my body and make it my slave so
that after I have preached to others, I myself will not be disqualified for
the prize.

1. *What was Paul's attitude toward preaching? Why? Do you feel that way about sharing the gospel? If not, why not?*

2. *What was Paul's model for preaching the gospel to those different from him? How should that apply to us?*

3. *What should the Christian do that is analogous to what an athlete does? Why?*

DAY FIVE READING AND QUESTIONS

Reread the entire text (8:1-9:27)

1. *What are some modern day parallels to "eating meat sacrificed to idols?" In other words, in our culture, what might we be free to do that would possibly cause others to stumble?*

2. *Paul went out of his way to make sure no one could lodge an accusation of self-promotion or self-profit in what he did for the Lord. Is this an example we should follow? If so, how?*

3. *Do you practice the spiritual disciplines regularly? Do you see yourself in training for an eternal reward? What can we do to encourage our brothers and sisters to train more actively in the Lord?*

MEDITATION

How do we make decisions concerning what we do? Do we consider the needs and feelings of those around us? Paul modeled this concern for others in an exemplary manner. Though there were things he unquestionably could have done with a good conscience before the Lord, he realized those very actions might mislead a weaker believer. Paul pleaded with the Corinthians to be mindful of such behaviors. Ultimately, living out Christ Jesus crucified meant they were to yield to the needs of others. It should mean the same for us. What of meat sacrificed to idols? Of course, that is not the question for us. But the principle certainly applies. Paul reminds us that, if we are carrying the cross, we first look to the spiritual well being of others. We should never allow the exercise of our rights to lead a struggling Christian to sin.

Paul went to great lengths to model this point, and he didn't limit it to not eating foods that might offend. In fact, at times it made life more difficult for him, but he would let nothing impede his ability to preach the gospel. While he certainly had the right to receive financial support for his teaching and preaching, for example, he chose not to do so. He did not want anyone thinking he was preaching for his own self-serving purposes. He simply had to preach! He was willing to do or become whatever he had to be in order to lead others to understanding God's grace. This is what we must hear. The purpose of our lives is to proclaim the gospel. The gospel is only proclaimed through those who carry the cross in what they do and say.

This way of self sacrifice for the sake of proclaiming God's message is not easy. Nor was it in Paul's day. Paul compared it to running a race against elite runners. All have trained diligently—only to receive a perishable prize. What about us? Should we expect to train any less? Think about the prize that awaits us—eternal glory! Does that not motivate us to train with great focus and desire? We must subject our bodies and minds to strict spiritual training for the sake of the gospel. Woe to us if we aren't proclaiming the good news of God to a broken and dying world!

"Lord Jesus, help us learn the way of the cross—dying to our own desires for the sake of others to the glory of God. May we devote our lives to strict spiritual training that we may be the spiritual athletes you have called us to be."

LEARN FROM ISRAEL

(10:1-11:1)

DAY ONE READING AND QUESTIONS

[1] For I do not want you to be ignorant of the fact, brothers, that our
forefathers were all under the cloud and that they all passed through the
sea. [2] They were all baptized into Moses in the cloud and in the sea. [3] They
all ate the same spiritual food [4] and drank the same spiritual drink; for
they drank from the spiritual rock that accompanied them, and that rock
was Christ. [5] Nevertheless, God was not pleased with most of them; their
bodies were scattered over the desert.

[6] Now these things occurred as examples to keep us from setting our
hearts on evil things as they did. [7] Do not be idolaters, as some of them
were; as it is written: "The people sat down to eat and drink and got up to
indulge in pagan revelry." [8] We should not commit sexual immorality, as
some of them did—and in one day twenty-three thousand of them died.
[9] We should not test the Lord, as some of them did—and were killed by
snakes. [10] And do not grumble, as some of them did—and were killed by
the destroying angel.

[11] These things happened to them as examples and were written
down as warnings for us, on whom the fulfillment of the ages has come.
[12] So, if you think you are standing firm, be careful that you don't fall!
[13] No temptation has seized you except what is common to man. And
God is faithful; he will not let you be tempted beyond what you can bear.
But when you are tempted, he will also provide a way out so that you can
stand up under it.

1. *Why do you think Paul reminded the Corinthians of the wilderness wanderings of the Israelites?*

2. *What sin did Paul want to make sure they did not repeat?*

3. *According to Paul, are there temptations so great they cannot be resisted? Why or why not?*

DAY TWO READING AND QUESTIONS

14 Therefore, my dear friends, flee from idolatry. 15 I speak to sensible
people; judge for yourselves what I say. 16 Is not the cup of thanksgiving
for which we give thanks a participation in the blood of Christ? And
is not the bread that we break a participation in the body of Christ?
17 Because there is one loaf, we, who are many, are one body, for we all
partake of the one loaf.

18 Consider the people of Israel: Do not those who eat the sacrifices
participate in the altar? 19 Do I mean then that a sacrifice offered to an
idol is anything, or that an idol is anything? 20 No, but the sacrifices of
pagans are offered to demons, not to God, and I do not want you to be
participants with demons. 21 You cannot drink the cup of the Lord and
the cup of demons too; you cannot have a part in both the Lord's table
and the table of demons. 22 Are we trying to arouse the Lord's jealousy?
Are we stronger than he?

1. *What was the connection between the Lord's Supper and the sin of idolatry, according to Paul?*

2. *What was the meaning of the cup, according to Paul? The loaf?*

3. *In what way might the Corinthians participate with demons? How might we do so?*

DAY THREE READING AND QUESTIONS

23 “Everything is permissible”—but not everything is beneficial. “Everything is permissible”—but not everything is constructive. 24 Nobody should seek his own good, but the good of others.

25 Eat anything sold in the meat market without raising questions of conscience, 26 for, “The earth is the Lord’s, and everything in it.”

27 If some unbeliever invites you to a meal and you want to go, eat whatever is put before you without raising questions of conscience. 28 But if anyone says to you, “This has been offered in sacrifice,” then do not eat it, both for the sake of the man who told you and for conscience’ sake— 29 the other man’s conscience, I mean, not yours. For why should my freedom be judged by another’s conscience? 30 If I take part in the meal with thankfulness, why am I denounced because of something I thank God for?

1. *Rather than seeking our own good, what are we to do? Why?*

2. *What should determine what one eats if eating at an unbeliever’s house?*

3. *With what attitude should every meal be taken, according to Paul? Is this the attitude with which you eat?*

DAY FOUR READING AND QUESTIONS

31 So whether you eat or drink or whatever you do, do it all for the glory of God. 32 Do not cause anyone to stumble, whether Jews, Greeks or the church of God— 33 even as I try to please everybody in every way. For I am not seeking my own good but the good of many, so that they may be saved. 1 Follow my example, as I follow the example of Christ.

1. *For what should we do all things?*

2. What does this mean? Provide some specific examples.

3. In what, according to these verses, are we called to follow Paul's example?

DAY FIVE READING AND QUESTIONS

Reread the entire text (10:1-11:1)

1. Do you see the story of Israel's unfaithfulness in the wilderness as a teaching example to you? Why or why not?

2. Paul tells us that what happened to the Israelites is recorded as examples and warnings to us. Do we teach the Old Testament stories in this way? How can we do this more effectively?

3. What influence does the Lord's Supper have on your thinking throughout the week? What do you think Paul would want us to consider as a result of sitting at the Lord's table?

MEDITATION

The story of Israel is great instruction for believers. Paul used their failure to be faithful to God as a warning to the Corinthians. Israel was punished because of their idolatry, and Paul wanted the Corinthians to avoid falling into that same sin. Idolatry was no small thing. It has always led and will always lead to destruction.

It is sobering to remember the great blessings Israel had been given and their refusal to accept those gifts. God freed them from inescapable slavery so that they might serve him and have life. Are we not living in a much greater blessing? Have we not been delivered from a more oppressive slavery? Is the cup of which we drink not a participation in that ultimate gift of being freed from our sins? Do we not feast on the loaf, thereby identifying ourselves as the body of Christ? These are the reminders Paul used to convince his readers to stay away from anything in this world that might hint of idolatry. He concluded his argumentation with the powerful charge, "whatever you do, do it all for the glory of God."

What, in our day, constitutes idolatry? Paul told the Corinthians they could not have a place at God's table and at the table of demons. Is it possible that we try to do just that? While meat sacrificed to idols is not on our tables, might lives given to earthly pursuits be around our tables? Is that not idolatry? What are we pursuing rather than God? Have we accepted the world's idea that the accumulation of wealth is where happiness and security is found? Do we eat at the table of narcissism and self-serving materialism during the week, and then sit at the Lord's Table on Sunday mornings thinking all is well? Why is that any different from what the Corinthians were doing?

Paul's challenge to center our lives on God's feast is helpful. It reminds us of the story into which we have been invited. We participate in the blood of Jesus every time we drink the cup. That moment is profoundly meaningful. We acknowledge our life has been purchased through the sacrifice of Jesus Christ. When we break the bread, we proclaim that we are participating in the body of Christ given to the world. Dare we take our bodies, purchased by Christ's blood and carrying his identity, to the feast table of false gods?

Our lives have one purpose. We are called to glorify God in everything we do. Paul was able to call his readers to follow his example in that very thing. Can we call others to follow our example in glorifying God?

"Dear Father, help us remember what you have done to save us and to fulfill our every need. May we look to you for strength to turn away from temptations and recognize our calling to glorify you in every thing that we do and say."

APPROPRIATE BEHAVIOR IN THE ASSEMBLY

(11:2-22)

DAY ONE READING AND QUESTIONS

2 I praise you for remembering me in everything and for holding to
the teachings, just as I passed them on to you.

3 Now I want you to realize that the head of every man is Christ, and
the head of the woman is man, and the head of Christ is God. 4 Every
man who prays or prophesies with his head covered dishonors his head.
5 And every woman who prays or prophesies with her head uncovered
dishonors her head—it is just as though her head were shaved. 6 If a
woman does not cover her head, she should have her hair cut off; and if
it is a disgrace for a woman to have her hair cut or shaved off, she should
cover her head. 7 A man ought not to cover his head, since he is the image
and glory of God; but the woman is the glory of man. 8 For man did not
come from woman, but woman from man; 9 neither was man created
for woman, but woman for man. 10 For this reason, and because of the
angels, the woman ought to have a sign of authority on her head.

1. *For what did Paul praise his readers?*

2. *Who is the head of every man? Why is this important in our understanding of life?*

3. *What was inappropriate behavior for the women of Paul's day? For the men?*

DAY TWO READING AND QUESTIONS

11 In the Lord, however, woman is not independent of man, nor is
man independent of woman. 12 For as woman came from man, so also
man is born of woman. But everything comes from God. 13 Judge for
yourselves: Is it proper for a woman to pray to God with her head uncov-
ered? 14 Does not the very nature of things teach you that if a man has
long hair, it is a disgrace to him, 15 but that if a woman has long hair, it is
her glory? For long hair is given to her as a covering. 16 If anyone wants
to be contentious about this, we have no other practice—nor do the
churches of God.

1. *Who is independent of whom in the Lord? Why is this significant?*

2. *According to the biblical story, how did woman come from man? Why is it significant that man is born of woman?*

3. *From whom does everything come? How does Paul use this in his argument?*

DAY THREE READING AND QUESTIONS

17 In the following directives I have no praise for you, for your meet-
ings do more harm than good. 18 In the first place, I hear that when you
come together as a church, there are divisions among you, and to some
extent I believe it. 19 No doubt there have to be differences among you to
show which of you have God's approval.

1. *How could meetings do more harm than good?*

2. *If a church suffers divisions, how is this evident when it assembles?*

3. *How might differences actually be a good thing?*

DAY FOUR READING AND QUESTIONS

[20] When you come together, it is not the Lord's Supper you eat,
[21] for as you eat, each of you goes ahead without waiting for anybody
else. One remains hungry, another gets drunk. [22] Don't you have homes
to eat and drink in? Or do you despise the church of God and humiliate
those who have nothing? What shall I say to you? Shall I praise you for
this? Certainly not!

1. *In what sense were the Corinthians not eating the Lord's Supper?*

2. *If one remained hungry and another got drunk, what does this tell us about the context of the Lord's Supper in the early church?*

3. *How could the church humiliate those who had nothing? It is possible for us to do this?*

DAY FIVE READING AND QUESTIONS

Reread the entire text (11:2-22)

1. *How can we show submission to Christ in the context of our culture? What are behaviors that might communicate a different message?*

2. *How can we live to the glory of one another so that God ultimately is glorified through us?*

3. *How can we avoid the danger of church gatherings being more harmful than good? What can we do to build a stronger sense of unity and love?*

MEDITATION

Paul felt it necessary to address confusion concerning appropriate behaviors when the church gathered. All behavioral problems are shaped to some extent by the particular cultural context, as is the case here. The cultural norm for a woman in a public assembly in Corinth was that she should wear a head covering. Apparently the women in the church were experiencing such freedom in Christ that as they prayed and prophesied, they were throwing off their head covering. Paul found this inappropriate conduct for the Christian women and counter to the purposes of the church assembly.

What do we make of such teaching in our churches today? Appropriate gender roles continue to be hotly debated. May I suggest a thought that has been helpful to me? Rather than arguing about specific attire or behavior, let's consider Paul's fundamental concern. We are to glorify God in every thing that we do. In Paul's time, the head covering and long hair were appropriate signs of submission to God for a woman in the church. Likewise, long hair on a man was a disgrace and signified a turning away from glorifying God. Clearly, today's customs do not attribute the same meaning to these particular hair styles or coverings. Paul's fundamental concern was that his readers recognize that everything comes from God and is for him. Any behavior that expressed a desire for self acclamation or made a statement of independence worked against God's call to community and interdependence. Such conduct was therefore inappropriate.

This is particularly important to us because we live in a world that highly values the independence of each individual. Having what we want when we want it, even at the expense of others' needs, is embraced as a necessity for meaningful life in our culture. In light of this, we who want to be followers of Jesus must constantly reflect on questions such as, "Am I doing all things to the glory of God and for the needs of others?" Or, "Am I behaving and dressing in a way that is consistent with a life fully submitted to God?" "Am I more concerned about the needs of others than my own personal wants and desires?"

"Lamb of God, take away my desire for self-glory. Continue to transform me into your image, that I might be a living sacrifice to the glory of God."

GATHERING AS CHRIST'S BODY AT HIS TABLE

(11:23-34)

DAY ONE READING AND QUESTIONS

[23] For I received from the Lord what I also passed on to you: The
Lord Jesus, on the night he was betrayed, took bread, [24] and when he had
given thanks, he broke it and said, "This is my body, which is for you; do
this in remembrance of me."

1. *Who had given Paul what he was now teaching?*

2. *Why does Paul reference the betrayal of Christ?*

3. *What does the bread of the Supper represent?*

DAY TWO READING AND QUESTIONS

[25] In the same way, after supper he took the cup, saying, "This cup is
the new covenant in my blood; do this, whenever you drink it, in remem-
brance of me." [26] For whenever you eat this bread and drink this cup, you
proclaim the Lord's death until he comes.

1. *What is the meaning of "new covenant" in the blood of Jesus?*

2. *What is a covenant? Do you often reflect on the covenant relationship you have with God through the blood of Jesus? Why or why not?*

3. *How does the eating of the bread and drinking of the cup proclaim the Lord's death?*

DAY THREE READING AND QUESTIONS

[27] Therefore, whoever eats the bread or drinks the cup of the Lord in
an unworthy manner will be guilty of sinning against the body and blood
of the Lord. [28] A man ought to examine himself before he eats of the
bread and drinks of the cup. [29] For anyone who eats and drinks without
recognizing the body of the Lord eats and drinks judgment on himself.
[30] That is why many among you are weak and sick, and a number of you
have fallen asleep. [31] But if we judged ourselves, we would not come under
judgment. [32] When we are judged by the Lord, we are being disciplined so
that we will not be condemned with the world.

1. *What is the "unworthy manner" of which Paul spoke?*

2. *What is there to examine before participating in the Supper?*

3. *In the context of the problems mentioned in 11:20, what is the lack of recognition of the body to which Paul referred?*

DAY FOUR READING AND QUESTIONS

[33] So then, my brothers, when you come together to eat, wait for
each other. [34] If anyone is hungry, he should eat at home, so that when
you meet together it may not result in judgment.

And when I come I will give further directions.

1. *Why do you think Paul concluded his teaching on the Lord's Supper with the instruction to "wait for each other"? How does that sum up his concerns?*

2. What did hunger have to do with Paul's concerns?

3. Why did Paul conclude by advising he would have more to say about this when he visited?

DAY FIVE READING AND QUESTIONS

Reread the entire text (11:23-34)

1. What does the bread of the Supper mean to you personally? How might it have more meaning?

2. What does the cup of the Supper mean to you personally? How might it have more meaning?

3. How could we effectively draw closer to one another in the observation of the Lord's Supper? How can we make it a more meaning proclamation of the Lord's death until he comes?

MEDITATION

Paul's discussion of the Lord's Supper is one of the better known sections of this letter. Central to the early church's assemblies and inaugurated as a feast of fellowship and unity, the Supper had unfortunately become another way for the Corinthians to express their individual status and privilege. The consequences to the church were devastating—weakness, sickness, even death (spiritual?). What had they done? They had forgotten the reason for breaking bread. They were to remember the body of the Lord. They were to remember their new covenant, with God and with one another, through the blood of Jesus. Their participation in the Supper was to proclaim the death of Jesus (the power of the cross) until his return.

These verses are often used to prepare the church for gathering at the table of our Lord, and appropriately so. Because of the manner in which most observe the Supper or communion in today's churches, Paul's concerns from verse 20 (in our last reading) do not make much sense to us. We do not struggle with members eating the Supper early, or with some eating much while others go hungry. Considering the size of the cups we generally use for the Supper, I cannot imagine anyone getting drunk, even if a church chooses to use wine. The early church observed the Supper as a part of a larger fellowship meal, which presented the opportunity for these particular issues to manifest themselves. But while we may not have the *same* excessive behaviors, might we still have the same basic thought patterns that led to such sins?

As we take the bread and cup, do we really remember? Do we truly discern the body of Christ Jesus? "Remember," as it is used by Paul, is a powerful word. It is much more than bringing to mind a past event. It calls us to participate in the event remembered for the purpose of redirecting our lives accordingly. "Remembering Jesus" means to recall *all* that he did—the purpose of his coming, the challenge of his calling, and the point of his death, burial and resurrection. It calls us, as a community, to be one in him. We are to discern his body, the church, of which we are one of many parts. If we allow ourselves to participate in the Supper with self-serving motives, unresolved conflicts, with a sense that we are more important than others in our assembly, how can this be a true remembrance of the one who died to make us one? This is a sacred moment of proclamation! The Lord died to make us his body. Let us eat the supper together. *Together*. As one. Only in this way will *we* (read: community) proclaim his death until he comes again.

"God of all creation, may we submit our lives to you so that all of our behavior reflects your glory. As we gather at your table, may our hearts and minds be one. May we remember, truly remember, the life, teachings, and death of Jesus. Redirect our hearts toward you that we might truly love one another."

SPIRITUAL GIFTS

(12:1-31a)

DAY ONE READING AND QUESTIONS

1 Now about spiritual gifts, brothers, I do not want you to be ignorant. 2 You know that when you were pagans, somehow or other you were influenced and led astray to mute idols. 3 Therefore I tell you that no one who is speaking by the Spirit of God says, "Jesus be cursed," and no one can say, "Jesus is Lord," except by the Holy Spirit.

4 There are different kinds of gifts, but the same Spirit. 5 There are different kinds of service, but the same Lord. 6 There are different kinds of working, but the same God works all of them in all men.

1. *Why do you think Paul wanted the Corinthians to understand the purpose and function of the spiritual gifts? What relationship would these gifts have to their former lives as pagans?*

2. *Why is it important to acknowledge different gifts in the church, but only one Spirit?*

3. *Paul taught the Corinthians that God was at work through the actions of each believer, when the body is functioning according to his will. Is this still true? If so, what do we need to do to better use the gifts of each member?*

DAY TWO READING AND QUESTIONS

7 Now to each one the manifestation of the Spirit is given for the common good. 8 To one there is given through the Spirit the message of wisdom, to another the message of knowledge by means of the same Spirit, 9 to another faith by the same Spirit, to another gifts of healing by that one Spirit, 10 to another miraculous powers, to another prophecy, to another distinguishing between spirits, to another speaking in different kinds of tongues, and to still another the interpretation of tongues. 11 All these are the work of one and the same Spirit, and he gives them to each one, just as he determines.

1. *What is the purpose of each spiritual gift?*

2. *Who is the source of the gifts within the church?*

3. *Who determines what each receives as a gift? Why is this important to acknowledge?*

DAY THREE READING AND QUESTIONS

12 The body is a unit, though it is made up of many parts; and though all its parts are many, they form one body. So it is with Christ. 13 For we were all baptized by one Spirit into one body—whether Jews or Greeks, slave or free—and we were all given the one Spirit to drink.

14 Now the body is not made up of one part but of many. 15 If the foot should say, "Because I am not a hand, I do not belong to the body," it would not for that reason cease to be part of the body. 16 And if the ear should say, "Because I am not an eye, I do not belong to the body," it would not for that reason cease to be part of the body. 17 If the whole body were an eye, where would the sense of hearing be? If the whole body were an ear, where would the sense of smell be? 18 But in fact God has arranged the parts in the body, every one of them, just as he wanted them to be. 19 If they were all one part, where would the body be? 20 As it is, there are many parts, but one body.

1. *Why was Paul so focused on emphasizing the idea of many parts yet only one body?*

2. *What was the problem of the foot and the ear in this illustration of Paul?*

3. *What is the purpose in the variety of gifts within the body of Christ?*

DAY FOUR READING AND QUESTIONS

21 The eye cannot say to the hand, "I don't need you!" And the head cannot say to the feet, "I don't need you!" 22 On the contrary, those parts of the body that seem to be weaker are indispensable, 23 and the parts that we think are less honorable we treat with special honor. And the parts that are unpresentable are treated with special modesty, 24 while our presentable parts need no special treatment. But God has combined the members of the body and has given greater honor to the parts that lacked it, 25 so that there should be no division in the body, but that its parts should have equal concern for each other. 26 If one part suffers, every part suffers with it; if one part is honored, every part rejoices with it.

27 Now you are the body of Christ, and each one of you is a part of it. 28 And in the church God has appointed first of all apostles, second prophets, third teachers, then workers of miracles, also those having gifts of healing, those able to help others, those with gifts of administration, and those speaking in different kinds of tongues. 29 Are all apostles? Are all prophets? Are all teachers? Do all work miracles? 30 Do all have gifts of healing? Do all speak in tongues? Do all interpret? 31 But eagerly desire the greater gifts.

1. *In this illustration, what was the problem of the self-assessment of the eye and of the head?*

2. *How is it that the parts of the body which are weaker are treated with special honor? What was Paul's point?*

3. *What is the normal reaction to injury to a particular part of our physical bodies? What should this teach us about how to respond to suffering and pain within the church?*

DAY FIVE READING AND QUESTIONS

Reread the entire text (12:1-31a)

1. *If you were to characterize your gifts as a part of the body, what would you be? An ear? An eye? A foot? A hand? Why? Do you feel you are a contributing part of the body of Christ?*

2. *How can we learn to be more interdependent in the church? What can we do to more effectively use the great variety of giftedness within our churches?*

3. *What can we do to honor those parts of the body of Christ that often feel unneeded or unappreciated because they are not gifted in the more visible ways (such as teachers, ministers, etc)?*

MEDITATION

What a fascinating and challenging illustration of the church! It is like a body, beautifully designed by God to function interdependently. Each part of the body is gifted by the designer of the body for the common good of all parts. This is another of Paul's powerful calls to true community. While there are clearly many different gifts, all are united by the one Spirit who leads us to lay our gifts at the feet of God to his glory.

Unfortunately, our sinful nature works against such unity. It whispers in our ears that our specific gifts are to be used competitively, as an advantage over others. Our particular gifts set us apart from everyone else. They either give us a reason to feel superior or inferior, depending on how the world values our gifts and abilities.

Paul's analogy of the body is both humorous and painfully revealing. Can you imagine your foot talking to your hand? Has your ear been talking to your eye lately? While that image may make us smile, the words Paul gave those parts are hauntingly familiar. The foot and the ear suffer from inferiority complexes. They are neither beautiful nor valued—at least not like the hand and the eye. So, they withdraw from providing their needed contribution to the body. The eye, however, has another problem. Interestingly enough, the eye talks to the hand—a body part thought to be of special standing to the foot. But the eye, you see, is far superior to the hand—at least according the eye. Paul illustrates the ridiculous nature of comparative valuing in the church. Is any part more important than another? Does not every part have an important function? Where would the eye be without the hand? Where would the body be without the ear and the foot?

Here is a really important truth: God is the designer of the body (as well as the creator of it). It is our responsibility to honor every part and encourage each to function according to its God-given giftedness. We must not allow those who are not able to teach or lead in some visible way to think they are somehow of lesser importance. It is the responsibility of all the parts to honor all other parts of the body. It is often those who think they have the least to offer who contribute the greatest gifts. We are the body of Christ—each of us is an indispensable part. Rather than berate those who do not (cannot?) do what we do, we should shower them with honor for what they contribute to the body. It is the body of Christ. Even those gifted in obvious ways have no value apart from the body. An eye, as beautiful and functional as it might be, is of no value without a body.

"Creator God, we praise you for how you have created us for community. Help us see our Spirit-given contribution to the body and give us a willingness to give what we have that we might display the wisdom of your design for the church."

LOVE IS THE GREATEST GIFT

(12:31b-14:12)

DAY ONE READING AND QUESTIONS

And now I will show you the most excellent way.

1 If I speak in the tongues of men and of angels, but have not love,
I am only a resounding gong or a clanging cymbal. 2 If I have the gift of
prophecy and can fathom all mysteries and all knowledge, and if I have
a faith that can move mountains, but have not love, I am nothing. 3 If I
give all I possess to the poor and surrender my body to the flames, but
have not love, I gain nothing.

4 Love is patient, love is kind. It does not envy, it does not boast, it is
not proud. 5 It is not rude, it is not self-seeking, it is not easily angered,
it keeps no record of wrongs. 6 Love does not delight in evil but rejoices
with the truth. 7 It always protects, always trusts, always hopes, always
perseveres.

1. *If love is the most excellent way, what were less excellent ways for the Corinthians?*

2. *Why was love such an important manifestation of faith in Christ, according to Paul?*

3. *What strikes you most in Paul's description of love in these verses? Do you love in this way?*

DAY TWO READING AND QUESTIONS

8 Love never fails. But where there are prophecies, they will cease;
where there are tongues, they will be stilled; where there is knowledge,
it will pass away. 9 For we know in part and we prophesy in part, 10 but
when perfection comes, the imperfect disappears. 11 When I was a child,
I talked like a child, I thought like a child, I reasoned like a child. When I
became a man, I put childish ways behind me. 12 Now we see but a poor
reflection as in a mirror; then we shall see face to face. Now I know in
part; then I shall know fully, even as I am fully known.

13 And now these three remain: faith, hope and love. But the greatest
of these is love.

1. *How can it be that "love never fails"?*

2. *Why did Paul use prophecies, tongues, and knowledge as things that would pass away? Why were they particularly relevant to his argument?*

3. *How is love greater than even faith and hope?*

DAY THREE READING AND QUESTIONS

14:1 Follow the way of love and eagerly desire spiritual gifts, especially
the gift of prophecy. 2 For anyone who speaks in a tongue does not speak
to men but to God. Indeed, no one understands him; he utters mysteries
with his spirit. 3 But everyone who prophesies speaks to men for their
strengthening, encouragement and comfort. 4 He who speaks in a tongue
edifies himself, but he who prophesies edifies the church. 5 I would
like every one of you to speak in tongues, but I would rather have you
prophesy. He who prophesies is greater than one who speaks in tongues,
unless he interprets, so that the church may be edified.

1. *How should "following the way of love" impact everything else the church does?*

2. *Why did Paul propose that prophecy was more helpful than tongues?*

3. *What did Paul see as the purpose of the gifts?*

DAY FOUR READING AND QUESTIONS

6 Now, brothers, if I come to you and speak in tongues, what good
will I be to you, unless I bring you some revelation or knowledge or
prophecy or word of instruction? 7 Even in the case of lifeless things that
make sounds, such as the flute or harp, how will anyone know what tune
is being played unless there is a distinction in the notes? 8 Again, if the
trumpet does not sound a clear call, who will get ready for battle? 9 So it
is with you. Unless you speak intelligible words with your tongue, how
will anyone know what you are saying? You will just be speaking into
the air. 10 Undoubtedly there are all sorts of languages in the world, yet
none of them is without meaning. 11 If then I do not grasp the meaning
of what someone is saying, I am a foreigner to the speaker, and he is a
foreigner to me. 12 So it is with you. Since you are eager to have spiritual
gifts, try to excel in gifts that build up the church.

1. *What analogy did Paul use to explain the possible confusion caused by the gift of tongues? For what was Paul pleading?*

2. *What kind of words did Paul want spoken in the church? Why?*

3. *In what did Paul ask the Corinthians to try to excel?*

DAY FIVE READING AND QUESTIONS

Reread the entire text (12:31b-14:12)

1. *Few passages are read more often than Paul's description of love in 1 Corinthians 13. As familiar as it might be to you, what new insights have you gained concerning love through your meditative reading of this text?*

2. *Why did Paul see love as the greatest gift? Do we regard love in this way? Why or why not?*

3. *What can we do today to participate in the building up of the church? Be specific to your situation.*

MEDITATION

While one might argue over the nature and expression of the spiritual gifts in today's church, Paul left no room to be confused about what is most important. The answer to the unrest caused by the Corinthian believers' misuse of the gifts was to seek the greatest gift—love. If one does not love, one does not live. There is no action outside the context of love that has meaning in and of itself. No matter how great the gift, it is rendered meaningless if one is not motivated by love. However, if one truly loves, one's actions take on endless meaning.

Paul's description of love in these verses is truly inspiring. This passage is regarded by many as some of the most significant and beautiful prose ever written. Unconditional, self-giving love is an amazing and challenging concept! And it is distinctly different from what is generally identified as love. Paul described love as he had learned its meaning from Jesus Christ. Its full expression was missing in the Corinthian church. Rather than being patient and kind, the Corinthians were intolerant and accusatory towards one another. Authentic love allows for wrongs, and still gives without limit. Rather than participating in an envious competition for attention and power, love willingly backs out of the limelight and rejoices in the successes of others. As Paul described love, it was the answer to all of the woes in the Corinthian church. It is the answer to our woes as well. Wait—did we not identify the cross as the solution to the Corinthian conflict? Yes! But love and the cross are not two different solutions. The cross is the ultimate manifestation of authentic, unconditional love.

Do we love? Are we patient and kind, not envious or boastful, not proud? Do we turn away from anything that will dishonor another person or anything that could be understood as self-seeking? Do we turn from anger, refuse to remember offenses against us, and rejoice only in truth? Do we protect others, trust others, hope in God, and persevere? Can you imagine an entire community of faith living this way? Paul could. It can only happen through the Spirit of God indwelling his church. What a message such a church would communicate to a dark and sinful world!

"Loving Father, help us grow in our love for you and one another."

WORSHIP THAT EDIFIES

(14:13-40)

DAY ONE READING AND QUESTIONS

[13] For this reason anyone who speaks in a tongue should pray that he
may interpret what he says. [14] For if I pray in a tongue, my spirit prays,
but my mind is unfruitful. [15] So what shall I do? I will pray with my spirit,
but I will also pray with my mind; I will sing with my spirit, but I will also
sing with my mind. [16] If you are praising God with your spirit, how can
one who finds himself among those who do not understand say "Amen"
to your thanksgiving, since he does not know what you are saying? [17] You
may be giving thanks well enough, but the other man is not edified.

[18] I thank God that I speak in tongues more than all of you. [19] But in
the church I would rather speak five intelligible words to instruct others
than ten thousand words in a tongue.

[20] Brothers, stop thinking like children. In regard to evil be infants,
but in your thinking be adults. [21] In the Law it is written:

"Through men of strange tongues
    and through the lips of foreigners
I will speak to this people,
    but even then they will not listen to me,"
says the Lord.

1. *What was the purpose of saying "amen," according to Paul?*

2. *Why did Paul give more value to intelligible words than speaking in tongues?*

3. *Why did Paul accuse the Corinthians of thinking like children? In what way were they doing so?*

DAY TWO READING AND QUESTIONS

22 Tongues, then, are a sign, not for believers but for unbelievers;
prophecy, however, is for believers, not for unbelievers. 23 So if the whole
church comes together and everyone speaks in tongues, and some who
do not understand or some unbelievers come in, will they not say that
you are out of your mind? 24 But if an unbeliever or someone who does
not understand comes in while everybody is prophesying, he will be
convinced by all that he is a sinner and will be judged by all, 25 and the
secrets of his heart will be laid bare. So he will fall down and worship
God, exclaiming, "God is really among you!"

1. *What problem did speaking in tongues create in the assembly?*

2. *How did prophecy lay bare the secrets of a sinner's heart?*

3. *What would cause a nonbeliever to witness the presence of God among believers?*

DAY THREE READING AND QUESTIONS

26 What then shall we say, brothers? When you come together, every-
one has a hymn, or a word of instruction, a revelation, a tongue or an inter-
pretation. All of these must be done for the strengthening of the church.
27 If anyone speaks in a tongue, two—or at the most three—should speak,
one at a time, and someone must interpret. 28 If there is no interpreter, the
speaker should keep quiet in the church and speak to himself and God.

29 Two or three prophets should speak, and the others should weigh
carefully what is said. 30 And if a revelation comes to someone who is
sitting down, the first speaker should stop. 31 For you can all prophesy in
turn so that everyone may be instructed and encouraged. 32 The spirits of

prophets are subject to the control of prophets. [33] For God is not a God of disorder but of peace.

1. *According to Paul, what should determine what activities take place when the church gathers? What should all activities do?*

2. *What determined whether one speaking in tongues should be allowed to speak before the church?*

3. *How did Paul propose that prophecies be verified as authentic messages from God?*

DAY FOUR READING AND QUESTIONS

As in all the congregations of the saints, [34] women should remain silent in the churches. They are not allowed to speak, but must be in submission, as the Law says. [35] If they want to inquire about something, they should ask their own husbands at home; for it is disgraceful for a woman to speak in the church.

[36] Did the word of God originate with you? Or are you the only people it has reached? [37] If anybody thinks he is a prophet or spiritually gifted, let him acknowledge that what I am writing to you is the Lord's command. [38] If he ignores this, he himself will be ignored.

[39] Therefore, my brothers, be eager to prophesy, and do not forbid speaking in tongues. [40] But everything should be done in a fitting and orderly way.

1. *What do you sense was the basic problem Paul was addressing concerning the assemblies of the Corinthian church?*

2. *Why did Paul ask if the word of God originated with them? What was his point?*

3. *Ultimately, how did Paul want everything to be done in the assembly? Why?*

DAY FIVE READING AND QUESTIONS

Reread the entire text (14:13-40)

1. What was Paul's major concern in these verses?

2. What can we learn from this text about the purpose of our church assemblies?

3. Do our worship assemblies inspire "outsiders" who might be in attendance to proclaim "God is really among you"? Why or why not?

MEDITATION

What a fascinating glimpse into a first-century church gathering! Every believer came to the assembly with a desire to contribute to the spiritual growth of the church. Some were speaking in tongues, others prophesying, some interpreting the tongues. While all these were marvelous manifestations of the Spirit of God among them, they were not all necessarily beneficial to the assembled church. Paul wanted to make sure that all they did was for building up of all who were present. This was not a place for personal spiritual expression, but rather a place for growing in the knowledge of God together.

What a joy it must have been to come together and share new insights concerning the kingdom of God. Some came with a hymn, others with words of instruction, others manifesting special gifts from the Spirit. Paul's question was, "Is what you are bringing a contribution that will edify and strengthen all who are present?" The purpose of the assembly was and is to strengthen and build the church.

The new freedoms and expressions the Corinthian believers had discovered in Jesus Christ as Lord were causing some confusion and maybe even chaos when they came together to worship. Paul wanted to put things in order so that all might be strengthened and the Lord truly praised. He wanted outsiders who were in the assembly to hear the powerful and penetrating word of God. So there needed to be order as they assembled. They should take turns speaking, and carefully consider whether the messages shared were truly from God. God, Paul explained, is a God of peace, and this peace should be reflected in the assemblies.

What do we make of these passages? How do they speak to us? Unfortunately, they have often been used to suppress any spontaneity or free expression in our assemblies. Too many have carefully selected certain verses from this text to enforce their views of proper conduct in church assemblies. Endless arguments concerning whether supernatural gifts from the Holy Spirit are still present in the church or ideas about appropriate participation of women in the church have come out of these instructions of Paul. The true power of this text is too often lost in such arguments.

Step back with me view the bigger picture. The church in Corinth was suffering division. The message of the cross had gotten lost in the human pursuit of significance and power. Paul was calling the church to actively live out the cross and reclaim its identity as the community of peace God intended it to be. Though the church was struggling, it was not a lost cause. The believers were still gathering together with a great desire to contribute to the spiritual growth of the community. Paul reminded them they were to behave as a body—many different parts, all working together in their appropriate roles for the building up of the whole. For the body to benefit from the contribution of all, there needed to be appropriate order—not to limit participation but to receive full benefit from each contribution.

Do our churches today appreciate and encourage the full contribution of every part so the body can be truly strengthened? Wouldn't it be wonderful to have so many desiring to contribute to the building up of the church that we would need to set guidelines for organizing our assemblies for the benefit of all?

"Heavenly Father, thank you for the amazing gifts you have given us as your people. Give us wisdom to encourage all to contribute their gifts and insights to the building up of the church."

RESURRECTION!

(15:1-58)

DAY ONE READING AND QUESTIONS

1 Now, brothers, I want to remind you of the gospel I preached to
you, which you received and on which you have taken your stand. 2 By
this gospel you are saved, if you hold firmly to the word I preached to
you. Otherwise, you have believed in vain.

3 For what I received I passed on to you as of first importance : that
Christ died for our sins according to the Scriptures, 4 that he was buried,
that he was raised on the third day according to the Scriptures, 5 and that
he appeared to Peter, and then to the Twelve. 6 After that, he appeared to
more than five hundred of the brothers at the same time, most of whom
are still living, though some have fallen asleep. 7 Then he appeared to
James, then to all the apostles, 8 and last of all he appeared to me also, as
to one abnormally born.

9 For I am the least of the apostles and do not even deserve to be
called an apostle, because I persecuted the church of God. 10 But by
the grace of God I am what I am, and his grace to me was not without
effect. No, I worked harder than all of them—yet not I, but the grace of
God that was with me. 11 Whether, then, it was I or they, this is what we
preach, and this is what you believed.

1. *Why was Paul so concerned with maintaining the purity of the gospel?*

2. *What, according to Paul, was of first importance?*

3. *How could Paul, once a persecutor of the church, claim to be an apostle of that same church?*

DAY TWO READING AND QUESTIONS

[12] But if it is preached that Christ has been raised from the dead,
how can some of you say that there is no resurrection of the dead? [13] If
there is no resurrection of the dead, then not even Christ has been raised.
[14] And if Christ has not been raised, our preaching is useless and so is
your faith. [15] More than that, we are then found to be false witnesses
about God, for we have testified about God that he raised Christ from the
dead. But he did not raise him if in fact the dead are not raised. [16] For if
the dead are not raised, then Christ has not been raised either. [17] And if
Christ has not been raised, your faith is futile; you are still in your sins.
[18] Then those also who have fallen asleep in Christ are lost. [19] If only for
this life we have hope in Christ, we are to be pitied more than all men.

[20] But Christ has indeed been raised from the dead, the firstfruits of
those who have fallen asleep. [21] For since death came through a man, the
resurrection of the dead comes also through a man. [22] For as in Adam all
die, so in Christ all will be made alive. [23] But each in his own turn: Christ,
the firstfruits; then, when he comes, those who belong to him. [24] Then
the end will come, when he hands over the kingdom to God the Father
after he has destroyed all dominion, authority and power. [25] For he must
reign until he has put all his enemies under his feet. [26] The last enemy to
be destroyed is death. [27] For he "has put everything under his feet." Now
when it says that "everything" has been put under him, it is clear that this
does not include God himself, who put everything under Christ. [28] When
he has done this, then the Son himself will be made subject to him who
put everything under him, so that God may be all in all.

1. *Why was the message of Paul dependent on the resurrection of Christ?*

2. *Why would we appropriately be pitied if Christ were not raised, according to Paul?*

3. *How was Christ the "firstfruits" of those who have fallen asleep? What should this mean to us?*

DAY THREE READING AND QUESTIONS

29 Now if there is no resurrection, what will those do who are
baptized for the dead? If the dead are not raised at all, why are people
baptized for them? 30 And as for us, why do we endanger ourselves every
hour? 31 I die every day—I mean that, brothers—just as surely as I glory
over you in Christ Jesus our Lord. 32 If I fought wild beasts in Ephesus for
merely human reasons, what have I gained? If the dead are not raised,

"Let us eat and drink,
for tomorrow we die."

33 Do not be misled: "Bad company corrupts good character."
34 Come back to your senses as you ought, and stop sinning; for there are
some who are ignorant of God—I say this to your shame.

35 But someone may ask, "How are the dead raised? With what kind
of body will they come?" 36 How foolish! What you sow does not come
to life unless it dies. 37 When you sow, you do not plant the body that will
be, but just a seed, perhaps of wheat or of something else. 38 But God
gives it a body as he has determined, and to each kind of seed he gives
its own body. 39 All flesh is not the same: Men have one kind of flesh,
animals have another, birds another and fish another. 40 There are also
heavenly bodies and there are earthly bodies; but the splendor of the
heavenly bodies is one kind, and the splendor of the earthly bodies is

another. [41] The sun has one kind of splendor, the moon another and the
stars another; and star differs from star in splendor.

[42] So will it be with the resurrection of the dead. The body that is
sown is perishable, it is raised imperishable; [43] it is sown in dishonor, it is
raised in glory; it is sown in weakness, it is raised in power; [44] it is sown a
natural body, it is raised a spiritual body.

If there is a natural body, there is also a spiritual body. [45] So it is
written: "The first man Adam became a living being" ; the last Adam, a
life-giving spirit. [46] The spiritual did not come first, but the natural, and
after that the spiritual. [47] The first man was of the dust of the earth, the
second man from heaven. [48] As was the earthly man, so are those who are
of the earth; and as is the man from heaven, so also are those who are of
heaven. [49] And just as we have borne the likeness of the earthly man, so
shall we bear the likeness of the man from heaven.

1. *If there is no resurrection, what did Paul propose as the appropriate use of one's life?*

2. *What analogies did Paul use to describe the nature of our resurrection bodies? What is his point?*

3. *After we physically die, whose likeness will we then bear? Should this be important to us? Why?*

DAY FOUR READING AND QUESTIONS

[50] I declare to you, brothers, that flesh and blood cannot inherit
the kingdom of God, nor does the perishable inherit the imperishable.
[51] Listen, I tell you a mystery: We will not all sleep, but we will all be
changed— [52] in a flash, in the twinkling of an eye, at the last trumpet.
For the trumpet will sound, the dead will be raised imperishable, and we
will be changed. [53] For the perishable must clothe itself with the imper-
ishable, and the mortal with immortality. [54] When the perishable has

been clothed with the imperishable, and the mortal with immortality,
then the saying that is written will come true: "Death has been swallowed
up in victory."

55 "Where, O death, is your victory?
Where, O death, is your sting?"

56 The sting of death is sin, and the power of sin is the law. 57 But
thanks be to God! He gives us the victory through our Lord Jesus Christ.

58 Therefore, my dear brothers, stand firm. Let nothing move you.
Always give yourselves fully to the work of the Lord, because you know
that your labor in the Lord is not in vain.

1. *What cannot inherit the kingdom of God, according to Paul?*

2. *In what sense will death be swallowed up in victory? Do you often think about this ultimate victory? Why or why not?*

3. *How can we possibly know that our work in this world for God is not in vain?*

DAY FIVE READING AND QUESTIONS

Reread the entire text (15:1-58)

1. *How does the resurrection of Jesus Christ influence your thinking about life? Should it have a greater impact than it does? Consider setting aside a few minutes each day to contemplate the victory over death represented by the resurrection of Jesus.*

2. *How can we demonstrate the joy of our hope for resurrection to nonbelievers in a meaningful way?*

3. *Consider Paul's challenge to "stand firm" and "let nothing move you" based on our belief in resurrection. In what ways should the*

resurrection give us the strength to be unyielding to the influence of this world?

MEDITATION

Resurrection! What a wonderful thought! Life does not end in physical death. One's story does not come to an end when one's physical body fails. How can we possibly know this to be true? Because the heart of the gospel is that Jesus died for our sins, that he was buried, and that he was raised on the third day! Our sins are forgiven, and we too will be raised because Jesus was raised! He is the firstfruits, he is the guarantee. We, too, shall be raised!

But how can we know Jesus was raised? That was easy for Paul to defend—he had seen the risen Lord. To this day, Paul remains one of the greatest evidences of the resurrection of Jesus. How else can one explain the remarkable change in his life? Once a fierce persecutor of the church, he became its most fearless advocate. Paul made it clear that without the resurrection of Jesus Christ, the Christian faith would make no sense. In fact, he suggested that without the resurrection we might as well live a life of fleshly gratification—eat, drink, and be merry! If life comes to an end at death, why not?

The importance of belief in the resurrection cannot be overstated. It is an indispensable part of the story of our lives. It is something upon which we need to meditate daily. It reminds us that our lives have meaning beyond this world. To not intentionally affirm the resurrection leaves us toiling "under the sun", where the writer of Ecclesiastes reminds us all is vain and meaningless. But there is more to life than that "under the sun"—so much more! We will be changed, in the twinkling of an eye; the perishable will put on the imperishable! Praise God!

Christ has died and is risen. But he is coming again. At the point, all dominion, authority, and power will be fully subjected to him. All enemies will be put under his feet, the last of which is death itself. Until then, we have work to do! We eat together at his table to proclaim his death until that moment. We confidently walk out into our fallen world, inviting all powers and principalities to submit with us to the will of God.

We must not be deterred by those who do not understand the true purpose of life. We must live out of the victory given by our Lord Jesus Christ! Our lives mean something. They are a part of the work of the eternal God. "Therefore, my dear brothers and sister, stand firm. Let nothing move you. Always give yourselves fully to the work of the Lord, because you know that your labor in the Lord is not in vain."

"Sovereign Lord, how can we thank you for the hope we have in Christ Jesus? Thank you for making our lives full of purpose! Help us keep our hearts and minds on your plan for our lives. Thank you for our victory through Jesus Christ over death!"

FINAL INSTRUCTIONS AND SALUTATIONS

(16:1-24)

DAY ONE READING AND QUESTIONS

1 Now about the collection for God's people: Do what I told the
Galatian churches to do. 2 On the first day of every week, each one of you
should set aside a sum of money in keeping with his income, saving it up,
so that when I come no collections will have to be made. 3 Then, when I
arrive, I will give letters of introduction to the men you approve and send
them with your gift to Jerusalem. 4 If it seems advisable for me to go also,
they will accompany me.

1. *What did Paul instruct the Corinthians about "the collection?"*

2. *Why did Paul not want collections to be made on his arrival?*

3. *What do you think the "letters of introduction" were? What was their function?*

DAY TWO READING AND QUESTIONS

5 After I go through Macedonia, I will come to you—for I will be
going through Macedonia. 6 Perhaps I will stay with you awhile, or even
spend the winter, so that you can help me on my journey, wherever I
go. 7 I do not want to see you now and make only a passing visit; I hope
to spend some time with you, if the Lord permits. 8 But I will stay on at

Ephesus until Pentecost, 9 because a great door for effective work has
opened to me, and there are many who oppose me.

10 If Timothy comes, see to it that he has nothing to fear while he is
with you, for he is carrying on the work of the Lord, just as I am. 11 No
one, then, should refuse to accept him. Send him on his way in peace so
that he may return to me. I am expecting him along with the brothers.

1. *Why was Paul delaying his visit to Corinth until after he passed through Macedonia?*

2. *Why had Paul decided to remain at Ephesus for a while?*

3. *What were Paul's instructions concerning Timothy? What do you think he meant when he requested that they "send him on his way in peace?"*

DAY THREE READING AND QUESTIONS

12 Now about our brother Apollos: I strongly urged him to go to you
with the brothers. He was quite unwilling to go now, but he will go when
he has the opportunity.

13 Be on your guard; stand firm in the faith; be men of courage; be
strong. 14 Do everything in love.

15 You know that the household of Stephanas were the first converts
in Achaia, and they have devoted themselves to the service of the saints.
I urge you, brothers, 16 to submit to such as these and to everyone
who joins in the work, and labors at it. 17 I was glad when Stephanas,
Fortunatus and Achaicus arrived, because they have supplied what was
lacking from you. 18 For they refreshed my spirit and yours also. Such
men deserve recognition.

1. *Why do you think Apollos was reluctant to return to Corinth?*

2. *Paul instructed the Corinthians to do everything in love. Identify three concrete ways in your life to do everything in love.*

3. *What was the submission for which Paul called when he spoke of the household of Stephanas? What kind of recognition do you think Paul had in mind?*

DAY FOUR READING AND QUESTIONS

19 The churches in the province of Asia send you greetings. Aquila
and Priscilla greet you warmly in the Lord, and so does the church that
meets at their house. 20 All the brothers here send you greetings. Greet
one another with a holy kiss.

21 I, Paul, write this greeting in my own hand.

22 If anyone does not love the Lord—a curse be on him.
Come, O Lord!

23 The grace of the Lord Jesus be with you.

24 My love to all of you in Christ Jesus. Amen.

1. *How would you conclude this letter if you were Paul?*

2. *What does Paul emphasize in his conclusion?*

3. *How has Paul demonstrated his love for the Corinthian church?*

DAY FIVE READING AND QUESTIONS

Reread the entire text (16:1-24)

1. *What should motivate us to give?*

2. *What do you think Paul would want us to be on guard against in our lives today?*

3. *What stands out to you most as a result of this study of 1 Corinthians?*

MEDITATION

Paul, in concluding his letter, had one more question to answer—concerning the collection—and then he closed with a few "announcements." Sounds like church, doesn't it? The conclusions to the New Testament letters are important, however. They remind us that the New Testament authors were writing to real people in actual circumstances of life. Paul wanted the Corinthians to live the life to which they had been called. He was deeply disturbed at the divisions, the immorality, and the lack of understanding of the will of God within the church. But he was committed to making a difference—to calling them to repentance. He reminded them not only of their calling to live out the reality of the cross, but to live in the hope of the resurrection. So he wrote them a personal letter as a spiritual father to his struggling children in the faith. Surely no one can doubt his deep love for them, and it was for that reason that he was compelled to teach them, chide them, and attempt to direct them back to God. Paul was convinced there was no life outside of the love of Jesus Christ and he desperately wanted his children in the faith to live there.

What can we learn from Paul through this letter? Take time to review those things which impacted you most in your study of this text. What does it mean to consider one's life as a visible expression of the power of the cross? How do we envision our role as God's faithful interpreters of life? Can we call others to imitate our living out the cross of Christ in our lives? If moved to confront a brother or sister in the Lord with their sin, would we do so out of our love for them? I would hope and pray that we could end any such call to restored life as Paul did. "The grace of the Lord Jesus be with you. My love to all of you in Christ Jesus. Amen." Amen, indeed.

"Lord God, give us the courage to stand for truth. Give us the wisdom to effectively call our brothers and sisters living in ways that do not honor you back to life in Christ. May we live in the power of our crucified Lord, in the power of the cross, so that we can call others to follow our example in Jesus."

2 CORINTHIANS:

BEING A LIVING WITNESS TO THE CROSS OF JESUS CHRIST

THE SPIRITUALITY OF 2 CORINTHIANS

The occasion of 2 Corinthians was Titus' return to Paul after having visited Corinth at Paul's request. He brought news concerning how the believers had responded to Paul's insistence for repentance (perhaps in 1 Corinthians or in another letter). But whatever the specific situation, 2 Corinthians presents a clear picture of Paul dealing with a church struggling not only with sin but in their relationship with Paul himself. While Paul was greatly relieved to hear from Titus that the believers in Corinth had accepted his plea for repentance, dangers remained.

2 Corinthians is complimentary, conciliatory and confrontational. We encounter the great love Paul had for this church he founded, the joy he experienced because of their willingness to repent and his great concern because of sins which continued to distract them from God's purposes for their lives.

The following themes from this letter are particularly helpful to us as we learn how to more effectively minister to the needs of those we love:

Living in the "Jesus" Way

The power of Paul's message was not only in the truth he taught but in the life he lived. As in 1 Corinthians, he was able to expound on the "Jesus" way by referencing his own (Paul's) manner of living. He was willing to put all at risk, to suffer, and even die if necessary, to show all the "Jesus" way of life. He used his own example consistently to clarify what it meant to live in the power of the cross of Jesus Christ. He exposed the false teaching and life style of his opponents by explaining how his own life was consistent with what Jesus taught while theirs was not. With delicious and helpful irony, he demonstrated the accusation made against him was not only true, but was a reason to rejoice! Paul was *indeed* nothing, and it was that which gave him such power. It was the Jesus way.

We have no power to change lives if we do live fully in the gospel we proclaim.

Compelling Images of Ministry

Some of the most beautiful images of the Christian life are found in this letter. They affirm not only the high calling of God, but the reality of our own weaknesses. Paul calls us to be "the aroma" of Christ, life to some and death to others. We are not to be peddlers of the gospel, but those who carry it deep in our hearts. We are jars of clay holding a treasure beyond measure. While outwardly we are wasting away, inwardly we are being renewed day by day! Our earthly tent will be replaced heavenly clothing. We are to be ministers of reconciliation. We are co-workers with God! Make a special note of each of Paul images of ministry and reflect carefully on their meaing in your meditations.

Confronting Sin in Love

As in 1 Corinthians, Paul was not hesitant to confront sin in this letter. His primary concern, once again, was to lead the Corinthians to the full life for which God had redeemed them. He knew his confrontation would bring much pain as it had in past correspondence, but without it they would never experience a godly sorrow leading to repentance. In his dealing with their sins, note how Paul was quick to affirm the good he saw in them. His deep love and authentic concern is always evident, even as he confronted their wrongful behavior. He chose not to see them as enemies, but brothers and sisters whom he loved deeply.

Generous Living and Giving

Paul's challenge to the Corinthian church to give generously to the needs of the saints in Judea is a compelling picture of life. A text too often limited to a church's contribution, it was written to call the Corinthians to a life that imitated the generous love of God.

This letter reminds us of a truth evidenced throughout God's story. Spiritual renewal is never fully complete. There is no "arrival" to a place where distractions and temptations cease to attack God's people. 1 Corinthians called for repentance. It was a successful plea, as we see in 2 Corinthians. But the call for repentance was not finished, nor will it ever be in this world. That day will come! But until then, let us accept Paul's challenge to live in the Jesus way so that we might call others to faithful living in God's kingdom.

"Loving Father, guide us in our reading and meditating on these words of your servant Paul. May we be deeply moved by his passion, spiritually enriched by his teachings, and truly motivated to serve you more fully through this study."

THE FATHER OF COMPASSION

(1:1-24)

DAY ONE READING AND QUESTIONS

1 Paul, an apostle of Christ Jesus by the will of God, and Timothy
our brother,

To the church of God in Corinth, together with all the saints
throughout Achaia:

2 Grace and peace to you from God our Father and the Lord Jesus
Christ.

3 Praise be to the God and Father of our Lord Jesus Christ, the
Father of compassion and the God of all comfort, 4 who comforts us in
all our troubles, so that we can comfort those in any trouble with the
comfort we ourselves have received from God. 5 For just as the sufferings
of Christ flow over into our lives, so also through Christ our comfort
overflows. 6 If we are distressed, it is for your comfort and salvation; if
we are comforted, it is for your comfort, which produces in you patient
endurance of the same sufferings we suffer. 7 And our hope for you is
firm, because we know that just as you share in our sufferings, so also you
share in our comfort.

1. *Why do you think Paul identified God as the Father of compassion and comfort as he began his letter?*

2. *How did the sufferings of Christ flow over into Paul's life?*

3. On what was Paul's hope for the Corinthians based?

DAY TWO READING AND QUESTIONS

8 We do not want you to be uninformed, brothers, about the
hardships we suffered in the province of Asia. We were under great
pressure, far beyond our ability to endure, so that we despaired even
of life. 9 Indeed, in our hearts we felt the sentence of death. But this
happened that we might not rely on ourselves but on God, who
raises the dead. 10 He has delivered us from such a deadly peril, and
he will deliver us. On him we have set our hope that he will continue
to deliver us, 11 as you help us by your prayers. Then many will give
thanks on our behalf for the gracious favor granted us in answer to
the prayers of many.

1. Why do you think Paul wanted the Corinthians to know of his hardships?

2. How did suffering affect Paul's relationship to God?

3. For what did Paul want the Corinthians to pray concerning his group?

DAY THREE READING AND QUESTIONS

12 Now this is our boast: Our conscience testifies that we have
conducted ourselves in the world, and especially in our relations with
you, in the holiness and sincerity that are from God. We have done so
not according to worldly wisdom but according to God's grace. 13 For we
do not write you anything you cannot read or understand. And I hope
that, 14 as you have understood us in part, you will come to understand
fully that you can boast of us just as we will boast of you in the day of the
Lord Jesus.

15 Because I was confident of this, I planned to visit you first so
that you might benefit twice. 16 I planned to visit you on my way to
Macedonia and to come back to you from Macedonia, and then to have
you send me on my way to Judea. 17 When I planned this, did I do it
lightly? Or do I make my plans in a worldly manner so that in the same
breath I say, "Yes, yes" and "No, no"?

1. *In what way has Paul and his group demonstrated God's grace?*

2. *Of what does Paul suggest both he and the Corinthians will be able to boast of in the day of the Lord Jesus?*

3. *What is the "worldly manner" of planning of which Paul speaks?*

DAY FOUR READING AND QUESTIONS

18 But as surely as God is faithful, our message to you is not "Yes" and
"No." 19 For the Son of God, Jesus Christ, who was preached among you
by me and Silas and Timothy, was not "Yes" and "No," but in him it has
always been "Yes." 20 For no matter how many promises God has made,
they are "Yes" in Christ. And so through him the "Amen" is spoken by us
to the glory of God. 21 Now it is God who makes both us and you stand
firm in Christ. He anointed us, 22 set his seal of ownership on us, and put
his Spirit in our hearts as a deposit, guaranteeing what is to come.

23 I call God as my witness that it was in order to spare you that I did
not return to Corinth. 24 Not that we lord it over your faith, but we work
with you for your joy, because it is by faith you stand firm.

1. *In what sense is Jesus Christ God's "yes"?*

2. *What is the "Amen" of which Paul speaks?*

3. *By what can we stand firm?*

DAY FIVE READING AND QUESTIONS

Reread the entire text (1:1-24)

1. *Does the comfort you receive from God lead you to comfort others? Why or why not?*

2. *What would it look like for us, like Paul, to conduct ourselves toward others in holiness and sincerity from God?*

3. *Meditate a few moments on Jesus as the "yes" of all of God's promises. What promise of God is most meaningful to you at this moment?*

MEDITATION

"Praise be to the Father of compassion and the God of all comfort, who comforts us in all our troubles." Really? Was Paul calling us to praise the one who could keep us out of trouble, yet seems to constantly lead us into it? Well, what should we expect from the Father of Jesus Christ? Indeed, God is a God of comfort and compassion. But he is also a God who sent his Son to suffer and die so that we might live. Paul understood this, and was more that willing to embrace suffering for the sake of expanding God's kingdom. Right from the beginning of his letter, Paul was defending his authenticity as an apostle. He was sharing news of his deep suffering--not to receive pity or compassion from the Corinthians, but rather to establish that he was walking in the truth. Only through sharing in Christ's suffering can we fully experience his comfort and compassion. Paul reminds the Corinthians that life in Christ was not one of ease and worldly comfort.

Such an appeal stands in stark contrast to how the gospel is often presented in today's world. Would people respond positively to "good news" that would likely cause them to suffer? Isn't the good news all about us being fulfilled and happy and comfortable in this world? What does that have to do with the life and teaching of Jesus? Life is about being faithful to God in all things. Paul said he felt he was under the sentence of death because of his experiences, yet it was in this desperation that he found the consolation of God. The God who raises the dead can deliver us from any peril, if he so chooses. Do we, with Paul, live in such a place of faith? I fear our pursuit of the easy life has robbed us of an intimate relationship of trust in our God.

We can be confident of our faith in God, no matter what the circumstances. There are no ambiguities in the promises of God. All of them have been emphatically proven true in the life, teachings, death and resurrection of Jesus Christ. He is the "yes" to all of God's promises! That is why we can say "Amen" or "may it be so."

Paul challenged the Corinthian believers to be a part of God's lack of ambiguity. Paul refused to participate in the "wishy-washy" nature of the world. His sincerity could be seen in his insistence on standing firm in the Lord. His actions were determined by what he believed to be best for God's kingdom. Apparently, Paul's detractors were accusing him of acting in ways that benefited only him. But Paul could confidently say "it is God who causes me to stand firm in his will. I call him as my witness." Could we say the same?

"Lord God of all comfort, help me develop a heart a heart for you that allows suffering to deepen my faith in you. May I stand firm in your will, calling you as a witness to my desire to always do your will."

AUTHENTIC MINISTRY

(2:1-3:18)

DAY ONE READING AND QUESTIONS

1 So I made up my mind that I would not make another painful visit to you. 2 For if I grieve you, who is left to make me glad but you whom I have grieved? 3 I wrote as I did so that when I came I should not be distressed by those who ought to make me rejoice. I had confidence in all of you, that you would all share my joy. 4 For I wrote you out of great distress and anguish of heart and with many tears, not to grieve you but to let you know the depth of my love for you.

5 If anyone has caused grief, he has not so much grieved me as he has grieved all of you, to some extent—not to put it too severely. 6 The punishment inflicted on him by the majority is sufficient for him. 7 Now instead, you ought to forgive and comfort him, so that he will not be overwhelmed by excessive sorrow. 8 I urge you, therefore, to reaffirm your love for him. 9 The reason I wrote you was to see if you would stand the test and be obedient in everything. 10 If you forgive anyone, I also forgive him. And what I have forgiven—if there was anything to forgive—I have forgiven in the sight of Christ for your sake, 11 in order that Satan might not outwit us. For we are not unaware of his schemes.

1. *How did Paul express his love for the Corinthians in the letter to which he refers?*

2. *Who was Paul calling the Corinthians to forgive? Why?*

3. How might Satan "outwit" believers, according to this passage? What does this say about the importance of forgiving believers?

DAY TWO READING AND QUESTIONS

12 Now when I went to Troas to preach the gospel of Christ and found that the Lord had opened a door for me, 13 I still had no peace of mind, because I did not find my brother Titus there. So I said good-by to them and went on to Macedonia.

14 But thanks be to God, who always leads us in triumphal procession in Christ and through us spreads everywhere the fragrance of the knowledge of him. 15 For we are to God the aroma of Christ among those who are being saved and those who are perishing. 16 To the one we are the smell of death; to the other, the fragrance of life. And who is equal to such a task? 17 Unlike so many, we do not peddle the word of God for profit. On the contrary, in Christ we speak before God with sincerity, like men sent from God.

1. Why did Paul leave Troas for Macedonia?

2. How is it that the fragrance of Christ is life to some and the smell of death to others?

3. What do you think Paul meant by the phrase, "we do not peddle the word of God?"

DAY THREE READING AND QUESTIONS

1 Are we beginning to commend ourselves again? Or do we need, like some people, letters of recommendation to you or from you? 2 You yourselves are our letter, written on our hearts, known and read by everybody. 3 You show that you are a letter from Christ, the result of our ministry, written not with ink but with the Spirit of the living God, not on tablets of stone but on tablets of human hearts.

4 Such confidence as this is ours through Christ before God. 5 Not
that we are competent in ourselves to claim anything for ourselves, but
our competence comes from God. 6 He has made us competent as minis-
ters of a new covenant—not of the letter but of the Spirit; for the letter
kills, but the Spirit gives life.

7 Now if the ministry that brought death, which was engraved in
letters on stone, came with glory, so that the Israelites could not look
steadily at the face of Moses because of its glory, fading though it was,
8 will not the ministry of the Spirit be even more glorious? 9 If the
ministry that condemns men is glorious, how much more glorious is the
ministry that brings righteousness! 10 For what was glorious has no glory
now in comparison with the surpassing glory. 11 And if what was fading
away came with glory, how much greater is the glory of that which lasts!

1. *In what sense do you think Paul considered the Corinthian believers to be his letter of recommendation?*

2. *How is it that the letter kills, but the Spirit gives life?*

3. *What is no longer glorious compared to what had come in the Spirit?*

DAY FOUR READING AND QUESTIONS

12 Therefore, since we have such a hope, we are very bold. 13 We are
not like Moses, who would put a veil over his face to keep the Israelites
from gazing at it while the radiance was fading away. 14 But their minds
were made dull, for to this day the same veil remains when the old
covenant is read. It has not been removed, because only in Christ is it
taken away. 15 Even to this day when Moses is read, a veil covers their
hearts. 16 But whenever anyone turns to the Lord, the veil is taken away.
17 Now the Lord is the Spirit, and where the Spirit of the Lord is, there is
freedom. 18 And we, who with unveiled faces all reflect the Lord's glory,
are being transformed into his likeness with ever-increasing glory, which
comes from the Lord, who is the Spirit.

1. What was the hope to which Paul referred? Hope in what?

2. What was the veil that covered the heart "when Moses was read?"

3. How are we being transformed? Into what are we being transformed?

DAY FIVE READING AND QUESTIONS

Reread the entire text (2:1-3:18)

1. When someone truly repents, do you find it easy to forgive that person and affirm your love for that person? Why or why not?

2. Do you spread the aroma of Christ in your daily life? If so, how? If not, why not? What do you need to do differently so that others might know of him through you?

3. Are you experiencing a continual transformation towards the image of Christ? How do you see this happening in your life?

MEDITATION

Paul must have been very direct in the correspondence to which he referred in these verses. It was so severe, in fact, that he chose not to accompany the letter as he first thought he might. Rather, he would give the church a chance to set things right, so that when he came he could rejoice with them. He was not hesitant to share his deep suffering in writing such a letter. Yet, because of his great love for them, he had no choice but to write it—even knowing the grief it would bring them. Now, he could truly rejoice with them over their decision to make things right.

What insight into the heart of Paul! He was willing to put all at risk for the good of God's kingdom. His approach to writing and teaching are important for us to understand. He carefully wove his life into God's redemptive story. He chose to do that which would be consistent with what God had done for him. Do we live this way? Notice how he spoke of his agonizing decision to leave Troas and journey on to Macedonia as a portrayal of Paul's participating in Christ's triumphal procession! He envisioned himself in the victory parade as a proud captive of Christ, spreading his aroma everywhere he went. What a wonderful picture! Close your eyes and envision being a part of Christ's victory parade! Spreading the good news of the kingdom is nothing like a peddler selling his wares! No. It is an exciting opportunity to participate in the victory of the ages, bring life to those who would hear the message and manifesting that any other purpose for living brings the stench of death!

Would Paul need physical letters of recommendation as his distracters suggested? No! Why should he? He called the Corinthians to look around—to see those participating in the victory parade of Christ because of his teaching and guidance. What greater commendation could there be? He could confidently affirm his authenticity as an apostle because of the hearts of the believers, as they were ever more fully transformed into the image of God in Christ. This is truly glorious! Why would Paul seek the recommendation of humankind when he was involved in such glorious work in the Spirit of God?

There is much here for us to contemplate. Is our work affirmed by the "ink" of a human pen or is it affirmed by the Spirit of the living God? Surely we see our incompetence in proving our value by what *we* do. Why live under such the burden of human approval when we are called to participate in the glorious ministry of God? We have been freed from the burden of proving ourselves by a God who indeed is competent and calls us to be transformed. It is a continual transformation of glory. How do we do this? Read on, Paul would say.

"God of glory, help us see the incomparable glory of your calling. Nothing in this world could be so compelling or meaningful! May we allow you to weave the story of our lives into the glorious tapestry of your redemptive work in the world."

TREASURES IN JARS OF CLAY

(4:1-5:10)

DAY ONE READING AND QUESTIONS

[1] Therefore, since through God's mercy we have this ministry, we do
not lose heart. [2] Rather, we have renounced secret and shameful ways;
we do not use deception, nor do we distort the word of God. On the
contrary, by setting forth the truth plainly we commend ourselves to
every man's conscience in the sight of God. [3] And even if our gospel is
veiled, it is veiled to those who are perishing. [4] The god of this age has
blinded the minds of unbelievers, so that they cannot see the light of the
gospel of the glory of Christ, who is the image of God. [5] For we do not
preach ourselves, but Jesus Christ as Lord, and ourselves as your servants
for Jesus' sake. [6] For God, who said, "Let light shine out of darkness,"
made his light shine in our hearts to give us the light of the knowledge of
the glory of God in the face of Christ.

1. How did Paul view his ministry? Through what had he received it?

2. How is the image of Jesus Christ to be seen in us?

3. How are we to have knowledge of the glory of God?

DAY TWO READING AND QUESTIONS

[7] But we have this treasure in jars of clay to show that this all-
surpassing power is from God and not from us. [8] We are hard pressed on

every side, but not crushed; perplexed, but not in despair; [9] persecuted, but not abandoned; struck down, but not destroyed. [10] We always carry around in our body the death of Jesus, so that the life of Jesus may also be revealed in our body. [11] For we who are alive are always being given over to death for Jesus' sake, so that his life may be revealed in our mortal body. [12] So then, death is at work in us, but life is at work in you.

[13] It is written: "I believed; therefore I have spoken." With that same spirit of faith we also believe and therefore speak, [14] because we know that the one who raised the Lord Jesus from the dead will also raise us with Jesus and present us with you in his presence. [15] All this is for your benefit, so that the grace that is reaching more and more people may cause thanksgiving to overflow to the glory of God.

1. *What was the treasure to which Paul was referring?*

2. *What was the clay jar of which Paul spoke?*

3. *What, in Paul's mind, would cause thanksgiving to overflow to the glory of God? What should this motivate us to do?*

DAY THREE READING AND QUESTIONS

[16] Therefore we do not lose heart. Though outwardly we are wasting away, yet inwardly we are being renewed day by day. [17] For our light and momentary troubles are achieving for us an eternal glory that far outweighs them all. [18] So we fix our eyes not on what is seen, but on what is unseen. For what is seen is temporary, but what is unseen is eternal.

[1] Now we know that if the earthly tent we live in is destroyed, we have a building from God, an eternal house in heaven, not built by human hands. [2] Meanwhile we groan, longing to be clothed with our heavenly dwelling, [3] because when we are clothed, we will not be found naked. [4] For while we are in this tent, we groan and are burdened,

because we do not wish to be unclothed but to be clothed with our heavenly dwelling, so that what is mortal may be swallowed up by life. [5] Now it is God who has made us for this very purpose and has given us the Spirit as a deposit, guaranteeing what is to come.

1. *What was the inward renewal of which Paul spoke?*

2. *What was the glory for which Paul waited? Is this something you think about in your life?*

3. *Are you, with Paul, confident of your "eternal building?" Why or why not?*

DAY FOUR READING AND QUESTIONS

[6] Therefore we are always confident and know that as long as we are at home in the body we are away from the Lord. [7] We live by faith, not by sight. [8] We are confident, I say, and would prefer to be away from the body and at home with the Lord. [9] So we make it our goal to please him, whether we are at home in the body or away from it. [10] For we must all appear before the judgment seat of Christ, that each one may receive what is due him for the things done while in the body, whether good or bad.

1. *According to Paul, what was the "downside" of being in this world?*

2. *How does one live by faith and not by sight?*

3. *For whose pleasure should we live, according to Paul? Why? How does this shape your thinking concerning your life?*

DAY FIVE READING AND QUESTIONS

Reread the entire text (4:1-5:10)

1. *Do you view your role in God's work in this world as an expression of his mercy? Why or why not?*

2. *What causes you to lose heart? What, according to Paul, should keep us from losing heart? How can we encourage one another to not be discouraged?*

3. *Does Paul desire to be "away from the body and at home with the Lord" diminish the importance of his physical life? Why or why not?*

MEDITATION

How does one lose heart? How does one come to the point that ministry is no longer worth the pain? Paul would likely say it is when we are thinking of pleasing someone other than God. The idea of living to an audience of one can be very freeing. If we live in God's presence and through his power, we do not have to resort to using deception or distortion to accomplish our purposes. We are free to live in truth in the sight of God. We are not commending or preaching ourselves, but Jesus Christ as Lord. Some won't get it. Paul was subtly identifying those opposing him in Corinth as being blinded to the glory of God because of their hard hearts. But the principle applies to all—those who are seeking truth will recognize it when they see it lived out authentically. It is like light in a dark room. It is undeniable to those whose hearts are open to it. "Jesus Christ as Lord" is indeed the treasure of the ages!

Ironically, the treasure is not held in eternal, magnificent, indestructible containers. Not yet, anyway. For now, the treasure is in our fragile bodies—jars of clay in Paul's terms. What an amazing thought! The greatest treasure in the history of the world abides in my temporary body made of mud. Why? Who can doubt where the real power originates? Our weakness demonstrates the power to be in God alone. So, in our suffering, in our incompetence, in our inadequacy, we rejoice! Our old temporary tents will someday be transformed. Wrinkles? Eyesight failing? Body falling apart? This should mean nothing to us! We know that any temporary suffering is nothing compared to what will someday be ours in Christ. We do not lose heart because our lives are firmly in God's hands.

The importance of Paul's thinking here cannot be overstated. We simply do not have the strength to continue ministering to others by our own power. We will lose heart if trying to operate by our own strength and purposes. If we are serving others for our own sense of satisfaction or if we are serving others for self advancement—we will lose heart. Paul's solution to this is to remind us with the Corinthians that we are in a "no lose" situation. Our bodies can even be destroyed in death and it still won't change our standing with God. In fact, it will be for the better, for we will then be at home with the Lord.

This is not a call for us to escape the reality of this world by dreaming of that which is to come. Quite the contrary! Paul is reminding us that we can indeed fully engage in the suffering of this world because we know that we are about the indestructible work of God. We fix our eyes on the eternal so that we can live fully and meaningfully in this temporary world of suffering and pain.

"Sustaining Lord, keep our hearts turned toward you that we may never lose heart. May our anticipation of being with you fill us with a desire to be about your work in this world."

MINISTERS OF RECONCILIATION

(5:11-6:13)

DAY ONE READING AND QUESTIONS

11 Since, then, we know what it is to fear the Lord, we try to persuade
men. What we are is plain to God, and I hope it is also plain to your
conscience. 12 We are not trying to commend ourselves to you again, but
are giving you an opportunity to take pride in us, so that you can answer
those who take pride in what is seen rather than in what is in the heart.
13 If we are out of our mind, it is for the sake of God; if we are in our right
mind, it is for you. 14 For Christ's love compels us, because we are convinced
that one died for all, and therefore all died. 15 And he died for all, that those
who live should no longer live for themselves but for him who died for
them and was raised again.

1. *What does it mean to "fear the Lord?"*

2. *What did Paul identify as the cause for his actions? From whom did he learn this way of life?*

3. *How is it that all have died because Christ died for us? How do we show this?*

DAY TWO READING AND QUESTIONS

16 So from now on we regard no one from a worldly point of
view. Though we once regarded Christ in this way, we do so no longer.

[17] Therefore, if anyone is in Christ, he is a new creation; the old has gone, the new has come! [18] All this is from God, who reconciled us to himself through Christ and gave us the ministry of reconciliation: [19] that God was reconciling the world to himself in Christ, not counting men's sins against them. And he has committed to us the message of reconciliation.

1. *What does it mean to no longer regard people from a worldly point of view?*

2. *What does it mean to be a "new creation" in Christ?*

3. *What is "the ministry of reconciliation" to which we are called?*

DAY THREE READING AND QUESTIONS

[20] We are therefore Christ's ambassadors, as though God were making his appeal through us. We implore you on Christ's behalf: Be reconciled to God. [21] God made him who had no sin to be sin for us, so that in him we might become the righteousness of God.

[6:1] As God's fellow workers we urge you not to receive God's grace in vain. [2] For he says,

"In the time of my favor I heard you,
    and in the day of salvation I helped you."
I tell you, now is the time of God's favor, now is the day of salvation.

1. *In what sense are we ambassadors for God?*

2. *What was Paul begging the Corinthians to allow to happen with their lives?*

3. *How does one become "the righteousness of God"?*

DAY FOUR READING AND QUESTIONS

3 We put no stumbling block in anyone's path, so that our ministry will not be discredited. 4 Rather, as servants of God we commend ourselves in every way: in great endurance; in troubles, hardships and distresses; 5 in beatings, imprisonments and riots; in hard work, sleepless nights and hunger; 6 in purity, understanding, patience and kindness; in the Holy Spirit and in sincere love; 7 in truthful speech and in the power of God; with weapons of righteousness in the right hand and in the left; 8 through glory and dishonor, bad report and good report; genuine, yet regarded as impostors; 9 known, yet regarded as unknown; dying, and yet we live on; beaten, and yet not killed; 10 sorrowful, yet always rejoicing; poor, yet making many rich; having nothing, and yet possessing everything.

11 We have spoken freely to you, Corinthians, and opened wide our hearts to you. 12 We are not withholding our affection from you, but you are withholding yours from us. 13 As a fair exchange—I speak as to my children—open wide your hearts also.

1. *What had Paul done to commend himself to the Corinthians?*

2. *What was Paul's point in his comparative or paradoxical statements in verses 8-10?*

3. *Why did Paul accuse the Corinthians of not opening their hearts to him?*

DAY FIVE READING AND QUESTIONS

Reread the entire text (5:11-6:13)

1. *Do you see yourself as a minister of reconciliation? Why or why not?*

2. *Have you suffered hardships as a result of your faith? If so, how? What is your attitude towards suffering?*

3. *Does the work and message of Jesus Christ change the way you see people? Do you see people as you think God sees them? Why or why not?*

MEDITATION

The calling of God to each of us is compelling! In Jesus Christ, everything is indeed new. We are called to a life oriented towards others, encountering each person and situation through the cross of Jesus. Even when the actions of others hurt us deeply, we choose not to take the offence personally. There is much more at stake than our feelings. We die (our self-centeredness) with Jesus so that we might live for him. Through the death and resurrection of Jesus, we have been given new eyes. We no longer see the world through a self-centered perspective. That worldly point of view has been destroyed.

It was this kind of life that Paul desperately wanted the Corinthians to embrace. He did not need human commendation as his opponents apparently insisted. Rather, he authentically lived the life to which he called the Corinthians. The compelling love of Christ caused him to see everything differently. Jesus Christ had died to give life, how could Paul live in any other way? Through the death and resurrection of Jesus Christ, Paul had been reconciled to God. Now he, too, was a minister of reconciliation, an ambassador for God's kingdom. His only concern was that all be reconciled to God. It is to this ministry we have all been called—as co-workers with God!

What a thought! What could be more important than to be a co-worker (fellow worker) with the Creator of the universe? What could be more meaningful than partnering with the loving redeemer of humankind? This is our calling—today! *Today* is the day, Paul reminds us. This was the pattern and purpose of Paul's life that he held out as commendation. His life displayed a willing to suffer anything—even death—in order to fulfill his exalted calling to be a disciple of Jesus Christ.

Paul's view of his life was radically shaped by the gospel. He embraced hardship, suffering, and distress as what should be expected of a follower of Jesus. After all, is that not what Jesus Christ has done for him and for all of us? Paul therefore refused to allow difficulty in his life to keep him from living faithfully. He expected it.

"Merciful Father, give us the strength to embrace suffering as a part of your plan. Help us learn to trust you in all things, so that even in our sorrows we find hope, peace, and joy in you."

PURE JOY IN CHRIST

(6:14-7:16)

DAY ONE READING AND QUESTIONS

[14] Do not be yoked together with unbelievers. For what do righteousness and wickedness have in common? Or what fellowship can light have
with darkness? [15] What harmony is there between Christ and Belial?
What does a believer have in common with an unbeliever? [16] What
agreement is there between the temple of God and idols? For we are the temple of the living God. As God has said: "I will live with them and walk among them, and I will be their God, and they will be my people."

[17] "Therefore come out from them
    and be separate,
says the Lord.
    Touch no unclean thing,
        and I will receive you."
[18] "I will be a Father to you,
        and you will be my sons and daughters,
        says the Lord Almighty."

[7:1] Since we have these promises, dear friends, let us purify ourselves from everything that contaminates body and spirit, perfecting holiness out of reverence for God.

1. *Paul often encouraged interaction with non-believers in order to proclaim the gospel to them. Now he commanded the Corinthian Christians to not be yoked with unbelievers. What do you think he meant by this?*

2. *How should our identity as the temple of God influence our association with others?*

3. *According to Paul, why should we be holy?*

DAY TWO READING AND QUESTIONS

2 Make room for us in your hearts. We have wronged no one, we
have corrupted no one, we have exploited no one. 3 I do not say this to
condemn you; I have said before that you have such a place in our hearts
that we would live or die with you. 4 I have great confidence in you; I take
great pride in you. I am greatly encouraged; in all our troubles my joy
knows no bounds.

5 For when we came into Macedonia, this body of ours had no
rest, but we were harassed at every turn—conflicts on the outside, fears
within. 6 But God, who comforts the downcast, comforted us by the
coming of Titus, 7 and not only by his coming but also by the comfort
you had given him. He told us about your longing for me, your deep
sorrow, your ardent concern for me, so that my joy was greater than ever.

1. *On what basis did Paul call the Corinthians to make room in their hearts for him? What can we learn from this?*

2. *How could Paul express such confidence in a church that had messed up so often?*

3. *How had Titus brought comfort to Paul?*

DAY THREE READING AND QUESTIONS

8 Even if I caused you sorrow by my letter, I do not regret it. Though
I did regret it—I see that my letter hurt you, but only for a little while—

9 yet now I am happy, not because you were made sorry, but because
your sorrow led you to repentance. For you became sorrowful as God
intended and so were not harmed in any way by us. 10 Godly sorrow
brings repentance that leads to salvation and leaves no regret, but
worldly sorrow brings death. 11 See what this godly sorrow has produced
in you: what earnestness, what eagerness to clear yourselves, what indig-
nation, what alarm, what longing, what concern, what readiness to see
justice done. At every point you have proved yourselves to be innocent
in this matter. 12 So even though I wrote to you, it was not on account
of the one who did the wrong or of the injured party, but rather that
before God you could see for yourselves how devoted to us you are. 13 By
all this we are encouraged.

1. *Why did Paul not regret the sorrow his letter caused?*

2. *What is the difference between godly and worldly sorrow?*

3. *What encouraged Paul in the midst of his confronting the sin in the Corinthian church?*

DAY FOUR READING AND QUESTIONS

In addition to our own encouragement, we were especially delighted
to see how happy Titus was, because his spirit has been refreshed by all of
you. 14 I had boasted to him about you, and you have not embarrassed me.
But just as everything we said to you was true, so our boasting about you
to Titus has proved to be true as well. 15 And his affection for you is all the
greater when he remembers that you were all obedient, receiving him with
fear and trembling. 16 I am glad I can have complete confidence in you.

1. *What delighted Paul?*

2. *What had Paul told Titus about the Corinthian Christians?*

3. *How could Paul speak of such confidence in them when they obviously had so many problems as they attempted to live out their faith?*

DAY FIVE READING AND QUESTIONS

Reread the entire text (6:14-7:16)

1. *Do you think of yourself as the temple of God? Would this thought help you avoid sin in your life? Why or why not?*

2. *What can Paul teach us about confronting sin? What if such a confrontation causes sorrow? Why do you think Paul would advise in this matter?*

3. *Why do you think Paul is constantly expressing his love and admiration for the Corinthians? How does this help accomplish his purpose for writing his letters? What might we learn from this in confronting sin in others?*

MEDITATION

In what sense are we not to be yoked with an unbeliever? Paul was not prohibiting interaction with non-believers. He even wrote the Corinthians in his first letter that those who were married to unbelievers should stay married to them if at all possible. So in what kind of relationship is Paul calling us to not be equally yoked to non-believers? Remember that Paul had just described, with much passion, the life of suffering he had experienced as a follower of Jesus Christ. The life of an authentic follower of Jesus Christ is not easy! Such a life has a specific direction, radically different from that to which our world calls us. There is a law in Deuteronomy (22:10) which prohibits an ox and a donkey from being yoked to the same plough. It makes sense. Their mannerisms, attitudes, and actions are significantly different. So it is with those of us who believe. How can we be deeply connected to one going in the opposite direction? We are called to be the temple of God. That is a serious responsibility. We are called to continually purify ourselves from worldly contamination. Consider carefully any association you have in your life that would cause you to pursue worldly things rather than the purposes of God for your life.

I am moved by Paul's constant affirmation of a church with so many problems. I am convinced he was not attempting to manipulate with his words—he was sincere in expressing his love, gratitude, and confidence in the believers in Corinth. Yes, they had many problems, but they also had good hearts. His love for the believers forced him to directly confront their sin, knowing it would bring much sorrow. Yet he had no regrets, because he knew ultimately it would lead them to godly sorrow and repentance.

Is this how we confront sin? Do we have such a love for our brothers and sisters in Christ that we are willing to put that relationship at risk for their ultimate good? Do we confront sin in such a way that it leads to godly sorrow and repentance? It is important to ask what we desire to happen as a result of our confronting sin. I see in Paul a clear indication that he did not want to punish, but restore. And God accomplished just that through his faithful servant. Even in confronting sin, in Christ there is reason for pure joy.

"Loving Father, we humbly ask for wisdom and strength in making decisions that honor and glorify you. Especially as we consider the difficult situations in confronting sin, may we have the wisdom to lead the erring to repentance."

SOWING GENEROUSLY

(8:1-9:15)

DAY ONE READING AND QUESTIONS

8:1 And now, brothers, we want you to know about the grace that God has given the Macedonian churches. 2 Out of the most severe trial, their overflowing joy and their extreme poverty welled up in rich generosity. 3 For I testify that they gave as much as they were able, and even beyond their ability. Entirely on their own, 4 they urgently pleaded with us for the privilege of sharing in this service to the saints. 5 And they did not do as we expected, but they gave themselves first to the Lord and then to us in keeping with God's will. 6 So we urged Titus, since he had earlier made a beginning, to bring also to completion this act of grace on your part. 7 But just as you excel in everything—in faith, in speech, in knowledge, in complete earnestness and in your love for us—see that you also excel in this grace of giving.

8 I am not commanding you, but I want to test the sincerity of your love by comparing it with the earnestness of others. 9 For you know the grace of our Lord Jesus Christ, that though he was rich, yet for your sakes he became poor, so that you through his poverty might become rich.

1. *Out of what had the Macedonian churches given their gifts?*

2. *What caused them to be so generous? What had they done to have such generous hearts?*

3. *What motivation did Paul provide to encourage the Corinthian Christians to give generously? How does this thought influence your thinking about giving?*

DAY TWO READING AND QUESTIONS

10 And here is my advice about what is best for you in this matter: Last year you were the first not only to give but also to have the desire to do so. 11 Now finish the work, so that your eager willingness to do it may be matched by your completion of it, according to your means. 12 For if the willingness is there, the gift is acceptable according to what one has, not according to what he does not have.

13 Our desire is not that others might be relieved while you are hard pressed, but that there might be equality. 14 At the present time your plenty will supply what they need, so that in turn their plenty will supply what you need. Then there will be equality, 15 as it is written: "He who gathered much did not have too much, and he who gathered little did not have too little."

16 I thank God, who put into the heart of Titus the same concern I have for you. 17 For Titus not only welcomed our appeal, but he is coming to you with much enthusiasm and on his own initiative. 18 And we are sending along with him the brother who is praised by all the churches for his service to the gospel. 19 What is more, he was chosen by the churches to accompany us as we carry the offering, which we administer in order to honor the Lord himself and to show our eagerness to help. 20 We want to avoid any criticism of the way we administer this liberal gift. 21 For we are taking pains to do what is right, not only in the eyes of the Lord but also in the eyes of men.

1. *How were the Christians to "finish" their work of giving?*

2. *What is the "equality" of which Paul speaks? Should we be concerned about this in our own lives? If so, how?*

3. *What had Paul done to assure no one would criticize the distribution of the gifts collected? What can we learn from this?*

DAY THREE READING AND QUESTIONS

22 In addition, we are sending with them our brother who has often
proved to us in many ways that he is zealous, and now even more so
because of his great confidence in you. 23 As for Titus, he is my partner
and fellow worker among you; as for our brothers, they are representa-
tives of the churches and an honor to Christ. 24 Therefore show these
men the proof of your love and the reason for our pride in you, so that
the churches can see it.

9:1 There is no need for me to write to you about this service to the
saints. 2 For I know your eagerness to help, and I have been boasting
about it to the Macedonians, telling them that since last year you in
Achaia were ready to give; and your enthusiasm has stirred most of them
to action. 3 But I am sending the brothers in order that our boasting
about you in this matter should not prove hollow, but that you may be
ready, as I said you would be. 4 For if any Macedonians come with me
and find you unprepared, we—not to say anything about you—would be
ashamed of having been so confident. 5 So I thought it necessary to urge
the brothers to visit you in advance and finish the arrangements for the
generous gift you had promised. Then it will be ready as a generous gift,
not as one grudgingly given.

1. *How did Paul describe Titus? Why was this important?*

2. *How did the enthusiasm of those to whom Paul was writing influence others? What might we learn from this example?*

3. *Why did Paul want the Corinthians to have the collection taken before those coming for it arrived?*

DAY FOUR READING AND QUESTIONS

[6] Remember this: Whoever sows sparingly will also reap sparingly,
and whoever sows generously will also reap generously. [7] Each man
should give what he has decided in his heart to give, not reluctantly or
under compulsion, for God loves a cheerful giver. [8] And God is able to
make all grace abound to you, so that in all things at all times, having all
that you need, you will abound in every good work. [9] As it is written:

"He has scattered abroad his gifts to the poor;
his righteousness endures forever."

[10] Now he who supplies seed to the sower and bread for food will
also supply and increase your store of seed and will enlarge the harvest
of your righteousness. [11] You will be made rich in every way so that you
can be generous on every occasion, and through us your generosity will
result in thanksgiving to God.

[12] This service that you perform is not only supplying the needs of
God's people but is also overflowing in many expressions of thanks to
God. [13] Because of the service by which you have proved yourselves, men
will praise God for the obedience that accompanies your confession of
the gospel of Christ, and for your generosity in sharing with them and
with everyone else. [14] And in their prayers for you their hearts will go out
to you, because of the surpassing grace God has given you. [15] Thanks be
to God for his indescribable gift!

1. *Why should we not give reluctantly or under compulsion?*

2. *Why is God a generous giver to his children? What does he expect us to do with his generosity?*

3. *What is the indescribable gift we have received from God?*

DAY FIVE READING AND QUESTIONS

Reread the entire text (8:1-9:15)

1. *What does this passage teach us about meeting the needs of other believers?*

2. *Why should we give generously of what we have? What basic spiritual understanding does our attitude towards giving show?*

3. *How might we express the surpassing grace of God we have generously received? List some specific actions.*

MEDITATION

The example of the Macedonian churches is challenging and deeply moving. Though in deep financial distress, their joy in the Lord led them to give generously to others in need! They contributed beyond their ability to give. Entirely on their own, they pleaded with Paul for the *privilege* of giving to the needs of the saints in Judea. What a wonderful testimony to the power of the changed heart! What a radically different way of looking at life. The Macedonians understood that life was found in giving to others, not accumulating for self. How could they be so generous? Paul provides the answer. They first gave themselves to the Lord. A generous heart is the result of a surrendered life. The fallen ideas of possessing things for status, of accumulating things for security, or living for self—all these false understandings of life die at the cross of Jesus Christ.

Paul wanted the Corinthians to demonstrate the same spirit. He did not want to command them to give, but to invite them to give because they too understood the meaning of God's redemptive story. Here it is—this is our story, too—we have been given the amazing grace of our Lord Jesus Christ. He who was rich beyond measure, for our sakes became poor, that we through his poverty might become rich. How can we, given so much, not have generous hearts towards those who have less?

Today, one of the constant challenges of churches is to meet their operating budgets. I wonder if we don't approach the whole idea of giving from the wrong perspective. Hearts deeply affected and transformed by the radical gospel of Jesus Christ give by nature, not compulsion. Paul sees generous giving as a sign of true conversion. He sees it as an act of faith in God's provision. He also sees it as a participation in the generous nature of God. Please understand this is not a "health and wealth gospel." Paul's message is not, "Give and you'll receive back more than you ever had." It is not money that is promised in return for generous giving, it is righteousness. Paul assumes God will provide for our physical needs. God is the one who supplies the seed and the bread. We are distributors of his wealth. And the more we demonstrate our faithfulness in giving, the more we will have to give.

Our motivation for giving should not be based on a budget need. Giving should be our nature. Especially as we see the needs of others. If we have more than we need, and a brother or sister has less than they need, does it not make sense to give to that need? Unfortunately, our eyes have been blinded to obvious truth by the values of our culture. May we first give ourselves to the Lord Jesus Christ. At that point, everything changes. The cross empties us of our need to trust anything other than God. He is the giver of the seed and the bread. May we trust him enough to be liberal givers of his gifts.

"Generous Lord, you in your eternal wealth became poor that we might be rich. Thank you for your love and grace. May we in turn give generously as a witness to your life-changing love. Thank you for your indescribable gift!"

PAUL DEFENDS HIS MINISTRY

(10:1-11:15)

DAY ONE READING AND QUESTIONS

10:1 By the meekness and gentleness of Christ, I appeal to you—I, Paul, who am "timid" when face to face with you, but "bold" when away! 2 I beg you that when I come I may not have to be as bold as I expect to be toward some people who think that we live by the standards of this world. 3 For though we live in the world, we do not wage war as the world does. 4 The weapons we fight with are not the weapons of the world. On the contrary, they have divine power to demolish strongholds. 5 We demolish arguments and every pretension that sets itself up against the knowledge of God, and we take captive every thought to make it obedient to Christ. 6 And we will be ready to punish every act of disobedience, once your obedience is complete.

7 You are looking only on the surface of things. If anyone is confident that he belongs to Christ, he should consider again that we belong to Christ just as much as he. 8 For even if I boast somewhat freely about the authority the Lord gave us for building you up rather than pulling you down, I will not be ashamed of it. 9 I do not want to seem to be trying to frighten you with my letters. 10 For some say, "His letters are weighty and forceful, but in person he is unimpressive and his speaking amounts to nothing." 11 Such people should realize that what we are in our letters when we are absent, we will be in our actions when we are present.

1. *Of what war was Paul speaking when he wrote, "We do not wage war as the world does?"*

2. *Why should we take every thought captive to the obedience of Christ? What does this mean?*

3. *What was Paul's concern about his words in his letters versus his words when present with the Corinthians?*

DAY TWO READING AND QUESTIONS

12 We do not dare to classify or compare ourselves with some who commend themselves. When they measure themselves by themselves and compare themselves with themselves, they are not wise. 13 We, however, will not boast beyond proper limits, but will confine our boasting to the field God has assigned to us, a field that reaches even to you. 14 We are not going too far in our boasting, as would be the case if we had not come to you, for we did get as far as you with the gospel of Christ. 15 Neither do we go beyond our limits by boasting of work done by others. Our hope is that, as your faith continues to grow, our area of activity among you will greatly expand, 16 so that we can preach the gospel in the regions beyond you. For we do not want to boast about work already done in another man's territory. 17 But, "Let him who boasts boast in the Lord." 18 For it is not the one who commends himself who is approved, but the one whom the Lord commends.

1. *What did Paul see as the problem of those who were "commending themselves?"*

2. *Why did he choose not to engage with them in their desire to boast of their accomplishments (at this point of his letter)?*

3. *Ultimately, in whom or what did Paul boast?*

DAY THREE READING AND QUESTIONS

11:1 I hope you will put up with a little of my foolishness; but you are already doing that. 2 I am jealous for you with a godly jealousy. I promised you to one husband, to Christ, so that I might present you as a pure virgin to him. 3 But I am afraid that just as Eve was deceived by the serpent's cunning, your minds may somehow be led astray from your sincere and pure devotion to Christ. 4 For if someone comes to you and preaches a Jesus other than the Jesus we preached, or if you receive a different spirit from the one you received, or a different gospel from the one you accepted, you put up with it easily enough. 5 But I do not think I am in the least inferior to those "super-apostles." 6 I may not be a trained speaker, but I do have knowledge. We have made this perfectly clear to you in every way.

1. *What is a "godly jealousy" as opposed to an ungodly jealousy?*

2. *To what was Paul calling the Corinthians in his use of the imagery of a pure virgin presented to Christ?*

3. *Of what was Paul fearful concerning the Corinthians?*

DAY FOUR READING AND QUESTIONS

7 Was it a sin for me to lower myself in order to elevate you by preaching the gospel of God to you free of charge? 8 I robbed other churches by receiving support from them so as to serve you. 9 And when I was with you and needed something, I was not a burden to anyone, for the brothers who came from Macedonia supplied what I needed. I have kept myself from being a burden to you in any way, and will continue to do so. 10 As surely as the truth of Christ is in me, nobody in the regions of Achaia will stop this boasting of mine. 11 Why? Because I do not love you? God knows I do! 12 And I will keep on doing what I am doing in

order to cut the ground from under those who want an opportunity to be
considered equal with us in the things they boast about.
[13] For such men are false apostles, deceitful workmen, masquerading
as apostles of Christ. [14] And no wonder, for Satan himself masquer-
ades as an angel of light. [15] It is not surprising, then, if his servants
masquerade as servants of righteousness. Their end will be what their
actions deserve.

1. *What decision was Paul defending in these verses? How might this issue have been used against him by his adversaries?*

2. *Why would Paul not change his mind on this matter?*

3. *Who are the false apostles of whom Paul speaks?*

DAY FIVE READING AND QUESTIONS

Reread the entire text (10:1-11:15)

1. *What are the spiritual weapons available to us as we fight against the powers of Satan?*

2. *What can we learn from Paul in his attitude towards those who are bragging of their own standing through their accomplishments?*

3. *Have you ever suffered from having your good intensions interpreted wrongly? What did you do?*

MEDITATION

Status and boasting was of immense importance in the ancient world. Self promotion was not viewed with suspicion. It was, in fact, expected. Paul, by refusing to participate in such self endorsement, appeared weak and vulnerable. How would Paul respond? Using a military metaphor popular in his time Paul explained that his weapons were not of this world. He would demolish his opponents' arguments and pretensions using divine power. He challenged the Corinthians to do as he had done--to take every thought captive and subject it the authority or obedience of Christ. The Corinthians had fallen prey to the superficial arguments of Paul's critics. Paul called the believers to examine their arguments at a deeper level.

What might we learn from Paul's treatment of his attackers? His language was aggressive and his tactics cause today's readers some discomfort. At times harsh, at other times sarcastic, he made it clear he was deeply injured—not so much by the attacks as by the Corinthians' seeming unwillingness to stand for the truth. First, I think it is obvious that Paul was deeply invested in those he taught. He had a profound love and concern for them. He was not lashing out in a self-righteous defense of his honor; he was battling for the well-being of those whom he loved. When we are attacked by critics of our kingdom work, what is our primary concern?

Second, Paul was not hesitant to confront his adversaries. He knew their arguments and the danger they represented and did not waste words exposing the faulty nature of their teachings. He knew the cost of false teaching was too high to ignore. Again, are we willing to confront error out of our concern for those who might be misled?

Thirdly, and most helpful to me, is that as Paul confronted his critics, his defense was one that taught deeper truths. He refused to argue a particular point at the surface level. When his critics wanted to argue his lack of dependability on one proposed journey, Paul responded by appealing to the certainty of God through Christ and his commitment to live in the same way. Paul's detractors suggested he had no basis for commendation, so Paul reminded the Corinthians that the only commendation that meant anything was the approval of God manifested by a life of obedience. When Paul's enemies attacked his refusal to accept pay, Paul took the Corinthians back to the example of Jesus Christ and Paul's willingness to join him in the journey of self-denial for the good of others.

Paul's response was of such depth that to this day we have not mined all of its richness. Read back over this passage. Underline the teaching points. The enemy attacked, God's faithful servant used it as an opportunity to teach.

"All powerful God, give us wisdom when attacked by those who would attempt to discredit our work for you. May we see all situations of conflict as opportunities to teach."

PAUL'S SUFFERING—GOD'S GRACE

(11:16-12:10)

DAY ONE READING AND QUESTIONS

16 I repeat: Let no one take me for a fool. But if you do, then receive
me just as you would a fool, so that I may do a little boasting. 17 In this
self-confident boasting I am not talking as the Lord would, but as a fool.
18 Since many are boasting in the way the world does, I too will boast. 19
You gladly put up with fools since you are so wise! 20 In fact, you even put
up with anyone who enslaves you or exploits you or takes advantage of
you or pushes himself forward or slaps you in the face. 21 To my shame I
admit that we were too weak for that!

1. *What do you think Paul is attempting to do in these verses? Why is he doing this?*

2. *Why does he make it plain that here he is not talking as the Lord would?*

3. *Why is Paul using sarcasm in his argumentation? Is it effective? Is it appropriate?*

DAY TWO READING AND QUESTIONS

What anyone else dares to boast about—I am speaking as a
fool—I also dare to boast about. [22] Are they Hebrews? So am I. Are they
Israelites? So am I. Are they Abraham's descendants? So am I. [23] Are they
servants of Christ? (I am out of my mind to talk like this.) I am more. I
have worked much harder, been in prison more frequently, been flogged
more severely, and been exposed to death again and again. [24] Five times
I received from the Jews the forty lashes minus one. [25] Three times I was
beaten with rods, once I was stoned, three times I was shipwrecked, I
spent a night and a day in the open sea, [26] I have been constantly on
the move. I have been in danger from rivers, in danger from bandits, in
danger from my own countrymen, in danger from Gentiles; in danger in
the city, in danger in the country, in danger at sea; and in danger from
false brothers. [27] I have labored and toiled and have often gone without
sleep; I have known hunger and thirst and have often gone without food;
I have been cold and naked. [28] Besides everything else, I face daily the
pressure of my concern for all the churches. [29] Who is weak, and I do not
feel weak? Who is led into sin, and I do not inwardly burn?

1. *Why does Paul see the boasting in which he engages here as foolish? Are these not accomplishments or incidents of which he should be proud? Why or why not?*

2. *What do you think Paul wants to accomplish by listing his experiences of difficulty?*

3. *Why is it that in all of Paul's writings he speaks so rarely of the episodes he here lists?*

DAY THREE READING AND QUESTIONS

30 If I must boast, I will boast of the things that show my weakness.
31 The God and Father of the Lord Jesus, who is to be praised forever,
knows that I am not lying. 32 In Damascus the governor under King
Aretas had the city of the Damascenes guarded in order to arrest me.
33 But I was lowered in a basket from a window in the wall and slipped
through his hands.

12:1 I must go on boasting. Although there is nothing to be gained,
I will go on to visions and revelations from the Lord. 2 I know a man
in Christ who fourteen years ago was caught up to the third heaven.
Whether it was in the body or out of the body I do not know—God
knows. 3 And I know that this man—whether in the body or apart from
the body I do not know, but God knows— 4 was caught up to paradise.
He heard inexpressible things, things that man is not permitted to tell. 5 I
will boast about a man like that, but I will not boast about myself, except
about my weaknesses. 6 Even if I should choose to boast, I would not be
a fool, because I would be speaking the truth. But I refrain, so no one will
think more of me than is warranted by what I do or say.

1. *Why would Paul want to boast in things that demonstrated his weakness?*

2. *Why does Paul speak of himself in the third person as he describes his vision of God?*

3. *Why does Paul not boast for having been shown and told such marvelous things?*

DAY FOUR READING AND QUESTIONS

7 To keep me from becoming conceited because of these surpass-
ingly great revelations, there was given me a thorn in my flesh, a
messenger of Satan, to torment me. 8 Three times I pleaded with the

Lord to take it away from me. [9] But he said to me, "My grace is sufficient for you, for my power is made perfect in weakness." Therefore I will boast all the more gladly about my weaknesses, so that Christ's power may rest on me. [10] That is why, for Christ's sake, I delight in weaknesses, in insults, in hardships, in persecutions, in difficulties. For when I am weak, then I am strong.

1. *Why was Paul given a "thorn in his flesh?"*

2. *What was it that "the thorn" was to teach Paul?*

3. *In exchange for personal boasting, what did Paul receive?*

DAY FIVE READING AND QUESTIONS

Reread the entire text (11:16-12:10)

1. *How do you regard things you have accomplished or received? Are these reasons for boasting? Why or why not?*

2. *Is there anything for us to learn from Paul intentionally using arguments of which he was against (boasting in the flesh)?*

3. *How do you view your sufferings or your weaknesses? Can they be understood as gifts to help you depend on God's grace?*

MEDITATION

You can't help but feel Paul's discomfort in the direction his argumentation takes at this point in his letter. He did not want to boast about himself. Such behavior was foolish and Paul knew it. However, since his opponents were so bold in their self-exaltation, Paul engaged them on their chosen turf. Some suggest Paul was parodying their behavior. It is not unlike his response to a similar attack in Philippians 3. If Paul's opponents wanted to confront him on the issue of worldly accomplishments, if he chose to, he could defeat them all. But as in Philippians 3, Paul demonstrated that it was not in his accomplishments that he found any real meaning. In fact, he suffered their loss in order to find true life and purpose in something far more valuable—knowing Christ Jesus. A high value of self based on worldly accomplishments precludes the possibility of a meaningful relationship with Jesus Christ as Lord. If you are proud of who you are without Jesus Christ, why would you need him?

Paul's detractors boasted of their worldly importance in order to establish their teaching as authoritative. Whether by parody or simple engagement, Paul reminded the Corinthians (as those of Philippi mentioned above) that he could easily win the battle of boasting. More importantly, it was through this exercise of self boasting that Paul demonstrated how foolish it was. For in all that he had accomplished—far beyond anything his opposition could claim—it was only through his weaknesses that he encountered God. It makes sense, then, that ultimately Paul would only boast of his weaknesses. For only in his weakness could he acknowledge his need for God's strength.

When we look in the mirror, what or who do we see? Are we proud for what we have accomplished? Do we use such things to establish our credibility before others? Ultimately, in whose strength do we depend? Those who know us well—what would they identify as that about which we would boast? What do you think—wouldn't it be a good thing to do away with the introduction of Christian speakers based on their accomplishments instead of their service?

"Omnipotent God, may we see the foolishness of claiming status based on anything we can accomplish in this world. Give us a sense of our complete dependence on you, that we may boast only of Christ in us."

CONCERNS FOR THE CORINTHIAN CHURCH

(12:11-13:12)

DAY ONE READING AND QUESTIONS

[11] I have made a fool of myself, but you drove me to it. I ought to
have been commended by you, for I am not in the least inferior to the
"super-apostles," even though I am nothing. [12] The things that mark an
apostle—signs, wonders and miracles—were done among you with great
perseverance. [13] How were you inferior to the other churches, except that I
was never a burden to you? Forgive me this wrong!

[14] Now I am ready to visit you for the third time, and I will not be a
burden to you, because what I want is not your possessions but you. After
all, children should not have to save up for their parents, but parents for
their children. [15] So I will very gladly spend for you everything I have and
expend myself as well. If I love you more, will you love me less? [16] Be that
as it may, I have not been a burden to you. Yet, crafty fellow that I am, I
caught you by trickery! [17] Did I exploit you through any of the men I sent
you? [18] I urged Titus to go to you and I sent our brother with him. Titus
did not exploit you, did he? Did we not act in the same spirit and follow
the same course?

1. *What did Paul believe marked him as an apostle?*

2. *What did Paul want from the Corinthians?*

3. *Paul claimed that neither he nor his party had been a burden to the Corinthians. Of what was he speaking?*

DAY TWO READING AND QUESTIONS

19 Have you been thinking all along that we have been defending
ourselves to you? We have been speaking in the sight of God as those
in Christ; and everything we do, dear friends, is for your strength-
ening. 20 For I am afraid that when I come I may not find you as I want
you to be, and you may not find me as you want me to be. I fear that
there may be quarreling, jealousy, outbursts of anger, factions, slander,
gossip, arrogance and disorder. 21 I am afraid that when I come again my
God will humble me before you, and I will be grieved over many who
have sinned earlier and have not repented of the impurity, sexual sin
and debauchery in which they have indulged.

1. *What was the motivation behind everything that Paul did for the Corinthians?*

2. *Of what did Paul fear as he anticipated visiting the Christians in Corinth?*

3. *To what was Paul calling the believers?*

DAY THREE READING AND QUESTIONS

1 This will be my third visit to you. "Every matter must be estab-
lished by the testimony of two or three witnesses." 2 I already gave you
a warning when I was with you the second time. I now repeat it while
absent: On my return I will not spare those who sinned earlier or any
of the others, 3 since you are demanding proof that Christ is speaking
through me. He is not weak in dealing with you, but is powerful among
you. 4 For to be sure, he was crucified in weakness, yet he lives by God's

power. Likewise, we are weak in him, yet by God's power we will live
with him to serve you.

5 Examine yourselves to see whether you are in the faith; test
yourselves. Do you not realize that Christ Jesus is in you—unless, of
course, you fail the test? 6 And I trust that you will discover that we
have not failed the test. 7 Now we pray to God that you will not do
anything wrong. Not that people will see that we have stood the test
but that you will do what is right even though we may seem to have
failed. 8 For we cannot do anything against the truth, but only for the
truth. 9 We are glad whenever we are weak but you are strong; and our
prayer is for your perfection. 10 This is why I write these things when I
am absent, that when I come I may not have to be harsh in my use of
authority—the authority the Lord gave me for building you up, not
for tearing you down.

1. What is Paul's definition of power?

2. How were the Corinthians to test themselves?

3. For what was Paul given authority over the Corinthians?

DAY FOUR READING AND QUESTIONS

11 Finally, brothers, good-by. Aim for perfection, listen to my appeal,
be of one mind, live in peace. And the God of love and peace will be
with you.

12 Greet one another with a holy kiss. 13 All the saints send their
greetings.

14 May the grace of the Lord Jesus Christ, and the love of God, and
the fellowship of the Holy Spirit be with you all.

1. For what were the Corinthians to aim?

2. How were they to live? To greet each other? Why?

3. How could Paul end such a stern letter with a Trinitarian blessing?

DAY FIVE READING AND QUESTIONS

Reread the entire text (12:11-13:12)

1. If you were one of the Corinthian believers, and knew that Paul was coming a third time, how would you react to this letter?

2. What do you think happened in the church in Corinth as a result of this letter?

3. How do you think Paul would address you and your church if he were writing you in anticipation of a visit?

MEDITATION

By "being forced" by the Corinthians to engage in boasting, Paul demonstrated the only way to attain true and lasting significance. Dare we follow his lead? Actually, this might not be a bad exercise for us all. Take an inventory of all you have that might give you a sense of importance or accomplishment. List every thing. What, on that list, has lasting value? What do we have that will endure? Only our relationship to God through Christ Jesus and our relationship with others—these are the things that will last.

It is important that we do not miss what Paul did in these verses. He took the accusation of his opponents ("Paul is nothing") and affirmed it was indeed true. It fact, he was "proud" he was nothing. Because rather than emptying him of his authority, it was what gave him authority! It was the realization that he was nothing that paradoxically made him everything he could possibly be--a being of ultimate power and significance! Until we can say with conviction that we are nothing, ironically, we indeed *are* nothing. It is in our "nothingness" that we find the only source of meaningful and lasting worth--the love of God offered through Jesus Christ dwelling in us through the Holy Spirit. This is the message Paul wanted the Corinthians to hear.

Their response to his letter would determine his role in coming. If they heeded his call for repentance, he would come and rejoice with them over their life in Christ. If they were continuing in their sins, he would not spare them the pain of confrontation. He challenged them to examine themselves to see whether Christ was truly dwelling in them. For, as he said, he could do nothing against the truth. His authority from the Lord was for building them up --but he could not build if they would not stand for the truth and live in the truth.

His final blessing demonstrates his ultimate desire for the believers in Corinth—"May the grace of the Lord Jesus Christ, and the love of God, and the fellowship of the Holy Spirit be with you all." That is where true life is found. There is nothing Paul would not do to lead the believers to the realization of that blessing.

How do we respond to such a letter? Every time I read one of the New Testament letters I wonder what that author would write to me, if he knew my spiritual condition. The discipline of self-examination is one I desperately need. There is nothing vague about Paul's challenge—"examine yourselves to see whether you are in the faith; test yourselves." Is Christ in me? Am I a living witness to the way of suffering for the sake of God's kingdom? Do I embody the "yes" in all of God's promises for those around me? Am I the aroma of Christ? Am I being transformed daily closer to the image of Jesus Christ? Do I value the amazing treasure of Jesus Christ as Lord in my fragile body? Do I live in the assurance of having an eternal building not made with hands when my physical body dies? Am I a minister of reconciliation? Am I a generous and cheerful giver? In what or in whom do I boast? Am I willing to confront error in a way that leads people to deeper truths? There is yet much to learn.

"God of mercy, lead us deeper into your heart. May we experience the grace of the Lord Jesus Christ, and your love, and the fellowship of the Holy Spirit in ever increasing ways."